The Taste Signature® Revealed

The Power of Emotions behind Taste of Food & Drink Brands

Derek E. Roberts & Thornton D. Mustard

The Taste Signature® Revealed
The Power of Emotions behind Taste of Food & Drink Brands

First published in 2012 by
Ecademy Press 48 St Vincent Drive, St Albans, Herts, AL1 5SJ
info@ecademy-press.com
www.ecademy-press.com

Printed and bound by Lightning Source in the UK and USA
Designed and artworked by Neil Coe

Printed on acid-free paper from managed forests. This book
is printed on demand, so no copies will be remaindered or
pulped.

ISBN 978-1-907722-91-2

A CIP catalogue record for this book is available from the
British Library.

This book is available online and all good bookstores.

Purpose of this book

This book is an update and a revision of the Taste Signature® published by QEP Marketing Clinic's founder, Thornton Mustard, in 2003. It incorporates new information, analysis and insights gained from the last decade's experience, particularly in major global markets, to provide further value.

The aim of this book is to examine and demonstrate the various inter-related aspects of taste and the psychological impact and emotional meaning they have for consumers and how this can translate into competitive advantage for food and beverage brand owning companies and their senior management, particularly marketing personnel, plus all those interested in food and drink! It is not a technical or scientific study or paper as there is plenty of other material which has covered such aspects of taste in scientific detail. However, to our knowledge there is only minimal material which links emotions to taste – scientific or otherwise.

Examples and case studies quoted are based on our general work in the field. No client information is quoted due to confidentiality, only that which is in the public domain, usually as submissions for winning marketing awards.

The information in this book is derived from qualitative research over the last 25+ years conducted by QEP Marketing Clinic using our proprietary methodology and systems.

These insights are drawn from over 6,000 groups, each run on average for two hours in duration, amongst a total of well over 30,000 research respondents covering more than 4,000 different food and beverage existing brands, products or new product development concepts.

This experience has provided the authors with a wealth of practical insight and knowledge into understanding the emotions behind taste and delivering consumer preference from that understanding.

Finally, for more information and updated chapters, please visit the book's website www.thetastesignature.com which is hopefully a useful information resource.

Acknowledgements

Thanks to Julie, our extremely patient PA who tells us what we should be doing. Also the other members of the QEP Marketing Clinic team, both employees and associated helpers.

Thanks to the individuals who are existing clients and retired clients who reviewed drafts of the book. Most were unable to give testimonials due to their company's policy but we appreciate them for their helpful and constructive comments.

Thanks to all our clients, for without their support we could not have gained the knowledge and experience required to write this book.

Thanks to the individuals who contributed the most to our knowledge, the 30,000+ consumers who attended our research groups from Birmingham to Beijing, without whose input and the subsequent insight gained there would have been no book.

Above all, thanks to our respective spouses, Carlette and Reth for putting up with, supporting and encouraging our obsessive behavior!

About the Authors

Derek Roberts

Derek started his long and active career in FMCG marketing as a graduate trainee with Cadbury Schweppes. After a number of promotions he progressed to an international marketing role in Smith Kline Beecham (the precursor to GSK).

He then became NPD Director for Bass brewers, the UK's largest brewer. In this senior marketing role he led a team which originated, developed and launched several brands such as Eisberg non-alcoholic wine and Caffreys Ale, Carling Range Extensions and Staropramen premium lager – multimillion pound brands which have stood the test of time to this day.

In this latter role he became personally aware of the Marketing Clinic and recognized and actively used its unique methodology on several projects with success as a client.

Thornton Mustard

By his mid-thirties Thornton was Managing Director of Wrigley Chewing Gum in the UK. Previously he had been Head of New Products for Avon Cosmetics, Europe and Group Marketing Director of Cussons Imperial Leather. Encouraged by Unilever he founded The Marketing Clinic in 1984, the first market research consultancy to specialize exclusively in 'Understanding the basis of flavor and fragrance preference'.

He continuously created, developed and improved many unique interconnected research methodologies to understand, predict and provide taste guidance to many global food and drink brands.

Inspired by Coca-Cola and Mars, Thornton wrote the first book on the direct connection between emotions triggered by taste and food preference. *The Taste Signature®* which was extensively reviewed by The Financial Times in October 2003 has started a revolution in the way taste and flavor is evaluated and applied today.

About QEP Marketing Clinic

Based in the US and UK we are a food and drink market research company that helps large global brand owners to gain competitive advantage by understanding why and how consumers make their taste choices through emotional preference.

Our company has over 25 years' experience researching over 6,000 food and drink products, helping to gain consumer preference for companies globally such as Kraft, Coca-Cola, Kellogg's, PepsiCo, Mars and Diageo amongst others.

Consumer preference is constantly moving as the palate and belief/value structure change in relation to food and drink. By using proprietary qualitative and quantitative tools and methodology we are able to understand the positive and negative emotions in a product's taste and texture to deliver competitive advantage in existing and new brands.

For more information visit

www.qepmarketingclinic.com
www.thetastesignature.com
www.derekeroberts.com

QEP Marketing Clinic is the branded trademark of QEP Research Inc. and QEP Research Ltd.

Contents

Contents

Definitions

A brief explanation of some phrases which you will come across in the book.

Consumption Experience – The Journey of Taste from start to finish revealing a product's emotional and physiological delivery.

Need State – The motivation for the consumption occasion incorporating how, why, where, when and who with of a product's consumption.

Encounter – Where and how a product is first met in the consumer's lifetime.

Moreishness – The consumer's response by wanting and consuming more of a product.

Drinkability and Sessionability – The moreish equivalent in beverages.

Melt – When food reacts to chewing and temperature to move the taste and texture from one state to another.

QEP Shape of Taste® – A diagrammatic way of illustrating the impact of different impacts of tastes and texture from start to finish in a product.

QEP Taste Signature® – The Consumption Experience from start to finish, matching the tastes and textures delivery to their associated major emotional benefits.

PART ONE

Chapter One
The Power of Emotions

Summary

- Emotions are powerful and can vary by individual based on their own personal experiences to form their own 'Signature'

- These emotions are generated by the senses which contribute to the overall reward obtained from food and drink

- The problem is trying to link the emotional reward to flavor, taste and texture

- The purpose of this book is to demonstrate how this can be achieved and its usefulness to the brand owner

- This will be achieved by firstly showing how taste evolves, secondly by showing how to map taste and finally to measure the emotions of taste

Every individual has their own personal favorites. This could be an activity, location, pastime, object, hobby, sport, holiday, color or so forth – whatever provides personal pleasure and satisfaction. This delight is based on the emotional response generated by that circumstance, object or event. This may be anticipation, excitement, relaxation, peace, danger or more complex sets of emotions – experienced individually or shared with others. The key is that the reward in the experience is delivered by emotions generated.

These emotions are formed by a multitude of stimuli that set up the emotional response. Different senses are individually or collectively employed to capture information that produces the response.

If everything is 'just right' then the desired emotional response is experienced and felt. However, small variations in the stimuli can break the emotional contract and the reward can be diminished or even disappear. On the other hand, if enough of the key stimuli elements kick in and connect, the mind will recognize the pattern and the experience 'Signature' and familiar feelings are now formed even if the context of the experience is quite different.

As previously stated, these responses are generated by the senses. Sight is obviously the dominant vehicle for gathering information and experiences are held as mental images in the picture of the mind. Sound can stir the emotions as well, in the form of favorite music or similar, while touch is also very important – the weight, temperature, smoothness, even rough texture can provide detailed information. Aroma is less direct and can be potentially elusive but most can recall and be stirred by the smell of freshly mown grass – even if to avoid hay fever!

Overall, sight, sound, touch and aroma can all contribute to the emotional reward in consuming a food or drink. However, it is the taste (flavor and texture) which can be the most difficult to identify and understand.

When describing taste, most consumers can only come up with half a dozen or so inadequate descriptors such as sweet, sour, salty, bitter and so forth. However, when a food or beverage producer tries to link these descriptions to emotional reward and thereby preference, the lack of vocabulary increases the problem exponentially.

However, in the forthcoming chapters we will show how such a vocabulary can be generated in order to understand and analyze the emotions behind taste preference so that food and beverage manufacturers can improve the appeal of existing brands/products and help develop new ones.

To do so, the book is divided into three parts. In Part One we begin by taking an overview of taste, its journey and how it evolves. We will then dig deeper looking at the Learnt Behavior of Taste and how it is acquired, developing the individual's taste palate. In particular we examine the pivotal role of the Encounter – how and when a taste is first met and its impact.

We progress from the Encounter – showing how taste develops and alters during our various life stages, particularly the huge transition that is represented by the teenage years.

Against this background we examine the growing influences of Culture and Fashion (changes in the perceived culture and value structure). One of the key influences is the growing Health and Wellness momentum amongst food and beverages plus its adversary – Obesity.

To complete the first part of the book we examine the increasing effect of Globalization on an individual's taste palate

In Part Two we examine the actual Journey of Taste. How taste and its various components work from start to finish in a QEP Consumption Experience®.

To do this we show how taste and its associated emotional delivery are impacted by the initial Appearance and Aroma, through to showing how different flavors impact the different parts of the mouth. We then move through to the Aftertaste and introduce the concept of Moreishness – why the consumer will want to consume more of a product versus the opposite – Satiation. In this chapter we will show how products can improve their particular Moreishness, plus the associated Sessionability, Drinkability, Refreshment and the opposite of Moreishness – Satiation.

Mouthfeel and Texture play an essential role in understanding this journey. A prime example of this is a phenomenon we refer to as the Melt – where it is present, the Melt is a major source of emotional delivery.

Finally, in Part Three we show how exactly you can measure the emotions of taste, through Need State categorization and understanding, to mapping and understanding the Taste Signature® and its importance and use in helping food and beverage brand owners achieve competitive advantage.

Throughout the book we also list a number of category examples as illustrations at the end of some of the chapters.

From the above we hope to demonstrate that Taste and its associated emotional journey is not just a given in a product, but a component that can be measured, mapped and improved in order to deliver consumer delight and satisfaction – Preference!

Chapter Two

The Changing Taste Palate

Summary

- The taste palate is changing and its rate of change is increasing

- This is due to a number of forces such as globalization, the influx of 'ethnic' foods, health and wellness and the rise of fast food

- The result is that many older, well-established products are becoming seen as 'not of today'

- Sometimes minor product modification can help dramatically

- However, often major NPD/reformulation is required to avoid a slow lingering death

The taste palate is changing rapidly and dynamically on a global basis, particularly in major international markets in the West and East.

The growth of air travel has allowed the freedom for consumers to explore new taste experiences. Alongside this there has been a major growth in international brands, particularly driven from the US but also European countries.

Conversely, we have also seen major growth in the use of more exotic imports, usually of a stronger spice nature, in the West which have become staple items in the diet: Mexican food in the US; curry in the UK; Chinese food everywhere! Alongside these stronger, more intense foods soft drinks have also become more intense and characterful in flavor; Red Bull is an example.

Meanwhile, the phenomenon that is fast food has seen a staggering increase, offering cheap, convenient, high-fat, high-taste meals. In contrast, we have also seen the growth of health and wellness food and drink which often reduce fat, sugar and salt – and therefore taste – as a major reaction to some of the above-mentioned food and drink.

The net result of this is that the current generation, particularly the young, is exposed to more and more different food and drink tastes and emotions compared to their parents' generation. Therefore, many 'old foods' are seen as old-fashioned and not of today and thus not for 'me'!

As an example, how many 20-year-olds drink Scotch and ginger ale? The answer is not many, as it is seen as an 'old man's drink' compared to Bourbon and Coke in most markets. The result is that many food and beverage brand owners struggle and seek to re-invigorate and develop their existing own brands, but how do they push back a trend that seems almost to be a force of nature?

Traditionally, these brand owners have often used the classic marketing tactics of trying (and not always succeeding) to reposition the brand through advertising, sponsorship or even just redesigning the packaging to appear more 'modern and relevant'. In addition, traditional market research methods and scoring of physical sensory attributes try to adjust and tweak tastes based on old paradigms and existing dimensions. The result is tactical marketing 'sticking plaster' on hemorrhaging brands which send the wrong emotional messages to the brand target market whose taste palate has moved on and left the brand behind. A classic example we worked on was a well-known chocolate countline which had been designed in the inter-war years as a tasty snack to fill a hunger need and provide energy. In the 21st century, a large part of their target market no longer worked in heavy manual labor and many, particularly young women, were leaving up to a third of the bar! This is a recipe for declining market share. Despite attempting the obvious tactical moves of offering smaller sizes and shapes, the brand still was declining across Europe.

Our work across Europe revealed amongst other aspects that the caramel layer in the bar was too intense and sticky for modern tastes, causing an almost caramel 'burn' in the throat plus the fondue part of the center lacked impact and was dominated by chocolate and particularly caramel. All this led to satiation and a feeling of a 'heavy' eat which was not relevant for the target market.

The result was that product modifications to the fondue and chocolate produced a bar more relevant to modern tastes. However, fundamentally a newer, lighter version of the bar was required which was subsequently developed.

Sometimes the taste palate of the consumer target market moves so far from the previous generations' that major new product development is required.

To try and pep up a 'tired' brand which does not reflect today's target market palate by advertising and repackaging merely endorses the same old tired brand and can even accelerate the brand's decline. All you are doing is reminding the target audience as to why they are rejecting the brand.

If the emotional messages derived from the taste or texture are negative, the harder you push, the more resistance is met. The consumer will reject the brand and it will die – often a slow, lingering and potentially expensive death.

Chapter Three

How Emotions of Taste are Initially Formed

Summary

- **Taste and its associated emotions are learned and developed over a lifetime**

- **From a young age, 'guidance' is obtained from parents and, potentially, older siblings**

- **The culture the child grows up in will be key to the guidance obtained**

Taste and the emotions derived are largely learned over the course of an individual's lifetime. From early childhood we are served taste in a controlled and largely sequential manner. The first taste we experience is mother's milk and for the rest of our lives any vanilla notes we experience in other foods will calm, relax and comfort.

Moving on from milk, a baby's diet is extraordinarily bland and diluted. Babies are incapable of accepting strong tastes. This could be derived from the sensitivity and relative number of taste buds or as an instinctive warning that their digestive system could not cope with such foods. Babies put an enormous number of different objects into their mouths, but instinctively know when to swallow and, thankfully, when not to swallow. It seems part of their learning experience is to put most small objects in their mouths and find out whether or not they are edible!

A lot of this 'guidance' is also from the parent who has an obvious enormous influence on the child's diet – both consciously and unconsciously forming the child's preference. Babies are highly sensitive to their parents' emotions and can read the expressions and body language of their parent like a skilled interrogator and are therefore influenced by the belief structure and diet of their parents –particularly their mother.

Similarly, faces and a sense of anticipated delight signal a yummy dessert while stern faces and a sense of force-feeding because it is 'good for you' signal cabbage – or even worse, Brussels sprouts!

Children are extraordinarily influenced by their parents in the diet they encounter which then can have a huge influence into adulthood. As a child grows older, the diet they encounter will start to become a pattern determined by their parents' own emotional preference and the society they grow up in. The balance between sweet, savory, salty, spicy, bland and creamy is fed to the child with a recommended emotional response which the parents themselves learned from their own childhood. Their child follows suit.

How, you may ask, is it that different children in the same family often develop different tastes? The answer is complex and not clear-cut but largely rests on the relationship between siblings and their respective positions in the family. Generally speaking, the firstborn is bred and trained for success but also with a sense of responsibility for their younger siblings. The middle order child has to fight for attention while the youngest is indulged. It is interesting to note that the US Air Force 'Top Gun' fighter pilot academy finds that younger siblings made better fighter pilots as they are prepared to take more risks, while older siblings take responsibility and are concerned about consequences.

So based on the parental attitude to their children, the attention and sequence of how different foods are introduced may vary accordingly.

In addition, younger siblings soon realize that often their attitudes and behavior in life have more in common with their older siblings than with their parents. The desire to copy and follow their older siblings is instinctive and constructive. However, there will come a time when the younger sibling will seek to differentiate themselves, particularly in their parents' eyes, which is reflected in the food they eat. Suddenly they will declare 'I don't like x food', mean it and adhere to it, possibly for the rest of their lives! Such behavior is complex to unwind as is most human behavior.

Of course, key to this evolution of taste is the culture the child grows up in and the influence of geography and climate. It is interesting to note that even in a small land mass such as the UK different regions have different taste palate preferences and behavior. This is increased in large geographic land masses such as the US, India and China. The influence of culture/geography and climate is dealt with later in the book – but its importance even in the light of increasing globalization cannot be underestimated.

Example of how a Product's Emotions and Physiology Deliver

Beer

Beer has an interesting history in that it came mainly from colder countries with an abundant supply of grain, unlike wine. These countries tended to have problems with the purity of water, so the best way to kill the bugs in water is to ferment and turn into alcohol. Consequently, the first historical choice of most of Northern Europe was to use beer as a form of liquid refreshment, developing a beer culture. When mass emigration occurred to the New World they took this beer culture with them. Part of this culture is that beer becomes part of the male rite of passage and a key component in male bonding in such cultures.

Traditionally, when the West was primarily a blue-collar manufacturing society the father used to take his 16-18-year-old (or even younger in some societies) to the local hostelry to have the son's 'first' beer. The problem is that to a young palate in teenage transition, used to sweet, fruity or milky cold beverages, beer tastes appalling! The first drink is dry, bitter with a strong and long-lasting sour aftertaste, never mind the strong, strange initial aroma allied to bloating and burping after-effects.

However, the social affirmation and the association of 'growing up' are very strong emotionally, both consciously and subconsciously, and this association stays with most men for the rest of their adult days. They literally learn to acquire the taste to gain the powerful emotional rewards. In the UK and Ireland the beer was likely to be dark, strong bitter or stout which took a long time – 6-24 months – for the hapless youth to acquire the taste. However, in the 1960s lighter, easier-drinking European-style lagers were introduced which were much more acceptable and their taste was easier to acquire and learn.

Nowadays, there is a plethora of global and regional easy-drinking, clean, crisp beers which are light and palatable, some drunk with a fashionable wedge of lime to cut through the bitterness even further. The first encounter with such beers is more likely to occur in a fashionable bar or club with the young adult's peer group. However, the social pressure to conform to the group is very powerful and failure to participate risks censure or even exclusion from the group – potentially very scary to a young male adult's confidence and self-image. Therefore, drinking the 'right' beer in the 'right' outlets is very powerful and important to the young drinker's image and self-confidence – very powerful emotionally but, like all things in the Teenage Transition, open to challenge and change. As the individual matures into adulthood, their palate can increasingly find such easy-drinking light beers unchallenging and lacking satisfaction – often 'too watery' in their own words. Furthermore, the beer is now thought 'immature' and OK for casual sunny BBQs but not for sessions in a pub or a bar. Increasingly, they will look for fuller flavor and mouthfeel initially, more demanding beers, even possibly reverting to the ales and stouts of their forefathers, but in the main stronger-tasting, drier and more sophisticated beers of any type which the brewers are happy to offer.

At first glance, being a brewer must be an easy ride compared to other food and drink brand owners. Once you appeal to the youth, you have the male adult for life, looking for different products from your product range in their lifespan. However, in the traditional western market strongholds consumption of beer has been on a steady decline for many years and increasingly the major brewery brand owners have had to look to the developing markets to retain their global sales. What is the reason for this decline? Although blue-collar manufacturing has declined in the western world and there is less call for replenishing the thirst and sweat from the working man, there are two other major factors which will also impact eventually on the developing markets. Wine and women!

Fundamentally, as beer has declined in traditional markets wine has grown in these areas. Wine's emotional values are calming, mellowing and relaxing whereas beer is refreshing, stimulating with some initial excitement and it could be argued that wine values are more in tune with dealing with the stress of modern living. However, the fundamental reason is that wine works much better with food. Its variants can be adapted and changed to suit different foods and ingredients. The state of the mouth after eating food and sipping wine is key to the product's success. It can wash away the harsher top notes of food while blending and enhancing the more complex food notes in the mid and rear mouth, as well as drying the mouth in the aftertaste, ready for the next mouthful of food. Beer, apart from working well with spicy and salty food, overpowers the lighter notes in food. It does not complement and clashes with the more complex notes in heavier foods, the bitterness of beer acting in a completely different way from the dryness of wine and not complementing the food. Some brewery brand owners have tried to design beers to suit food with limited success, although some of the more exotic Belgian beers have enjoyed success with some foods – mussels for example –but generally the physiological and emotional barriers are too great to displace wine's role with food.

In addition, wine is starting to take beer's place as an informal and social drink without food. The reason is that women are increasingly the opinion formers in the choice of drink in the household. Most women find beer too challenging. Although very refreshing, its sour aroma, potential frothy 'moustache', high volume, bitterness and bloating mitigate against its appeal. Brewers designing a 'beer for women' such as making a lighter, less gassy, even sweeter beer will fail to address the fundamental emotional and physiological barriers to women.

Wine, on the other hand, is one of women's first choices of alcoholic drink at an early age, usually accompanied by food, perhaps in a female setting; it can then be taken to informal social functions and appeal to both sexes. Men tend to follow their partners in their choices and will continually share a bottle and find it interesting and acceptable for most occasions, locations and with different company. Indeed, men often become so enthusiastic for wine that they displace their partner as the wine enthusiast and drive the purchase.

Beer therefore faces an uphill battle to convince women and serving it in a fancy bottle or glass is not going to change the dominance of wine as a first choice in most social and informal occasions. The highlight of many a married couple's week is sharing a bottle of wine in front of the TV once the children are in bed. Beer cannot compete with this emotional relief!

Chapter Four

Taste – an Overview

Summary

- **The Consumption Experience of a food or beverage is a journey**

- **This journey triggers over a hundred conscious and unconscious feelings and sensations**

- **It is difficult for consumers to adequately articulate and express these feelings and sensations**

- **In addition, people's tastes constantly change reflecting their age and lifestyle**

- **The consumer's selection of preferred tastes reflects these emotional values**

The Consumption Experience is a journey. It starts with the eyes, is investigated by the nose, evaluated and re-evaluated by taste and texture through the mouth until swallowed. It then leaves an aftertaste plus significant emotions and even a physiological reaction in the after-effects.

This convoluted journey, triggering over a hundred conscious and unconscious thoughts and feelings, is complex and can have a major impact on people's daily lives. However, it is extremely difficult for most people to express these emotions of taste; the classic reaction is 'nice' with maybe a bit of an explanation on the sweet, sour, salty axis. It is possible that this inadequate description and lack of vocabulary is down to our caveman reaction to anything poisonous or decaying, our instinct for danger overriding the niceties of description – which becomes a low priority. Whatever the explanation, there is undoubtedly a huge disconnect between the enjoyment of the eating experience and our ability to communicate adequately our joy or displeasure at the experience.

Today we enjoy many new foods and tastes from anywhere in the world. As the launch of a new product becomes increasingly more expensive for the brand owner, current brands have to be exploited but also utilize and fit into these abundant new tastes and textures, otherwise the brand is seen as 'old-fashioned' by today's generation and loses the brand's historical meaning.

Taste is constantly changing and reflects its time. Ingredients and the perception of recipes change constantly – almost becoming a fashion item, based on changing beliefs such as health and wellness. Are potatoes good or bad for you? Discuss! So how are the brand owners to evaluate taste and meet their new demands?

The learning of tastes and their meanings from childhood and adolescence, experimenting with flavors and tastes in their teens, the encounter with new foods, drinks and brands means that, over their lifetime, every adult builds up a whole series of taste preferences. These are usually based around raw ingredients which vary by growing process and processing by country to have a local interpretation influencing flavor and mouthfeel. Coffee, chocolate and tea have wide differences in flavor around the globe. Meat reflects feeding, climate and husbandry as do dairy products.

The ingredients in a recipe can be adulterated but tend to develop the core intrinsic flavor further. These flavors become learnt by society, becoming associated with the purpose and occasion they are used in and therefore mean the same to those consumers in an age cohort in that society. All of this becomes learnt opinion, differing by generation and slightly separated between men and women to form a taste palate.

However, this is not cast in stone. People do develop lifestyles and philosophies and these opinions directly affect the food and drink they consume. Changing beliefs impact and influence the acquired flavor and preferred choice. For example, those who have a commitment to a balanced diet often keep a constant if informal audit of what they are eating. This enables them to reduce the effect of indulging in fatty foods by consuming lighter, less sweet and rich foods – either before by 'buying' the indulgent occasion by 'being good' or subsequent behavior to mitigate guilt and restore balance.

Therefore many consumers bring to their food and drink consumption patterns, value judgments about how much or how little or how frequently certain foods should be consumed, causing them to critique tastes and mouthfeels. They then choose the available foods and drinks that reflect their beliefs on what they should or should not be consuming. What is happening is that taste selection is based on foods that support their emotional beliefs and are true to their values. These emotions, positive or negative, will largely determine what they eat or drink.

Chapter Five

Acquiring Taste

Summary

- As a child grows older, foods and drinks are increasingly presented with emotional attachments

- Some of these foods and their associated values are retained throughout an individual's lifetime

- The 'Teenage Transition' is a key time of experimentation with new tastes and experiences

- However, these values and experiences are often questioned and rejected in later adult life

- It is therefore difficult for an individual food or drink product to succeed throughout a person's life

As the child begins to grow older, so the foods are presented with attached emotions. 'This is fun, a treat, this is good for you, this will help you grow' and so forth. The child is already being influenced in its palate and the emotional meanings of some of the different flavors as well as the appropriate response in that culture.

When the child reaches four or five, the social context becomes more important through increasing birthday parties and Christmas and other festivities – the first celebrations. In order for a party to be successful, the vast majority of those attending must enjoy the food and drink – party food. In most cultures there are foods that are only eaten at parties. As the whole point of a party is to break with the everyday, to create fun and celebration, there must be specific party foods so these particular flavors become associated with party food – jell-o, trifle, and certain cakes. The adult equivalent is champagne in most cultures.

In the normal daily eating behavior, however, children tend not to like contrasting tastes and textures. Indeed, many eat the ingredients in a dish category by category in a predetermined order, which reinforces familiarity and reduces the power and challenge of the taste message. The alternative technique is to mix everything together into a homogenous mass which neutralizes stronger tastes and buries new ones.

From childhood the complexity of each taste and texture in the in-mouth experience is learned along with the associated meanings. Children, with their multitude of taste receptors, receive the maximum stimulus with minimal understanding. If the taste and texture is too challenging, complex or very new, they struggle to decode and process the food. That is why simple, unchallenging food is preferred, a blander alternative to the adult food which is soft, easy to eat, requires minimal eating and cutlery skills along with a minimum range of flavors. It is also stunningly repetitive. Some children enjoy a limited range of six or so items, served in various permutations, for years. Many men even continue to do this into adulthood, to the exasperation of their spouses and restaurant chains!

As examples of how certain foods retain their simplicity with children let's examine bread and ice cream versus yogurt and chocolate.

Children are more comfortable with the softness, blandness and ease of eating of white bread. Brown bread or wholegrain is too texturally demanding as children struggle with 'bits' – either real or slight – in anything.

Ice cream is a great food for children even though served cold. Flavors are unadventurous and secondary textures are off-putting and challenging. Yogurt's texture is soft and smooth with a subtle taste but its acidity can be challenging if not reduced in some child-friendly variants.

The universal favorite, chocolate, gives greater insight into the child's palate. So strong is the flavor that children can only handle mini portions of undiluted chocolate, or it has to be buffered by other ingredients. So a filled confectionery bar (say soft cookie) with an easy interior and a relatively low level of chocolate coating is ideal as the chocolate impact is diluted. Alternatively it can be presented in a milk mix shake or as a spread. Products such as Nutella dominate markets while chocolate cookies are popular in others. Textures are still soft and a true crunch and munch has not been developed.

As the child moves into adolescence and is able to select more of their own choices from the cupboard or buy items with pocket money, the selection is still comparatively limited and unadventurous. Children adore crunchy foods like chips or cereals but granular or gritty foods are still unpopular.

The taste palate remains stable until the 'Teenage Transition'. At first sight this appears to be triggered by puberty which accelerates the process, but it usually commences with the start of sixth grade (or UK secondary school) taking them from 11 or 12 years old until the start of adulthood. This is an environment driven by peer group structure and pressure, experimentation and the search for individual personality.

With increased experimentation, new ideas and experiences become very attractive, leaving many of the favorite childhood foods behind. However, if trouble is encountered in their teen group they will still reach for their old childhood favorites as a source of comfort.

By the time of the 'Teenage Transition', the taste buds are now organized into their adult format. The taste buds on the roof of the mouth and cheeks have disappeared whilst the taste buds on the tongue are now more specialized. For example, the tip of the tongue is now expert at detecting sweetness, while sourness is picked up at the side of the tongue, acidity is the pit of the tongue and bitterness at the back of the tongue and a little in the throat. This is the basis of how taste works in adult life.

Flavors can be manipulated so that the taste is extended in terms of impact but still operates in the confines of the now defined taste palate.

In a culture and environment which questions parental values, the teenager wishes to experience the world in their own way – but within the safety of the peer group. So their tastes are dominated by the behavior and the views of their friends and the need to conform to these views is very strong.

However, having rejected (at least in public) childhood foods so that familiar juice drinks and chocolate-covered biscuits can seem inappropriate as signaling safety and security, now risk and adventure become attractive. Anything new is amazing! Things of their parents' generation are boring!

Depending on the scale of rebellion, the teenager will choose foods and drinks their parents reject. The only inhibitors are flavor and money. However, in general terms the teenager is pretty pragmatic. They eat for fuel, especially boys, which they need in substantial quantities. Simple but distinct tastes are preferred. Cheese, previously only enjoyed in its mildest form, is now enjoyed in different strengths. Other strong flavors, such as sauces, are heavily used. Milk and cereals are very popular since they are fast-eating, snack-like in texture and have the milky comfort that can be useful.

Chocolate now starts to be enjoyed enthusiastically in various forms, delivering energy when needed as well as comfort and relaxation when required. When it is eaten containing cookie or other creamy, chewy centers, it mixes security with crunch and adventure to be attractive, approachable, initially exciting then calming and safe. These filled countlines of chocolate give bulk, bite and chew for greater satisfaction to the growing teenager than pure chocolate. Parental disapproval over the quantity eaten guarantees its popularity!

Once in their 20s, life now becomes more serious and individuals develop their own personal values. As the teenager left childhood products behind so does the adult reject the behavior of teenage years – often with cringing embarrassment. It is time to move on and enjoy more full-flavored and complex foods, drier and more sophisticated 'adult' food and recipes.

We can see how it is extremely difficult for a food and drink brand to succeed for all of a person's life on a consistent basis. Few brands can meet the requirements of childhood, move into the teenage years and then progress to adulthood. It has to metamorphose into another format, to be presented as a different entity and experienced and encountered in a new fashion.

Example of how a Product's Emotions and Physiology Deliver

Cider

Cider-making has a long history since Roman times but has generally been confined to a number of North European apple-growing areas such as the West of England and Normandy and Brittany in France. Since colonial times, the USA has had a history of cider-making but that had largely died out until fairly recently when there has been a tremendous growth in micro-craft cider production.

Essentially the drink is alcoholic, made from fermented apple juice and has an interesting, simple fruitiness with astringency from the apples' acidity and is usually served carbonated. This results in the mouth being cleansed and the fruitiness does not build up to be satiating; therefore it is crisply stimulating, refreshingly drinkable and sessionable.

Traditionally in the UK it was an entry point alcoholic drink for teenagers, often drunk from large bottles in parks in a group away from adult eyes. Initially it is an easy fruity drink that seemed close to soft drinks and as a result far too much was consumed, leading to most becoming sick. As they were vomiting, the acidity and astringency present in the cider seemingly increased and, along with the simple fruitiness, became fixed in the subconscious, the taste and subsequent memory paired together in the memory.

When the teenager became an adult and perhaps tried cider on a hot summer day, the subconscious memory would be triggered by the fruity aroma and acidity, making them feel childish. The powerful connection between taste and learnt emotion acted synergistically and produced a clear, memorable and embarrassing response. This held back cider-drinking in the UK for many years despite excellent efforts with the development of White Cider, which had more neutral wine notes; the beverage was only marginally successful.

However, the development of 'Alcopops' ready-to-drink, fruity carbonated beverages in the 1990s enabled cider's entry point to be replaced with an easier to acquire taste even closer to the learnt soft drink taste of their childhood. This meant that, as teenagers' first entry point into alcohol, such drinks were in turn eventually thought 'childish' by the maturing adult as they moved on to more sophisticated beverages.

This has opened the door to the re-emergence of cider as a popular adult beverage, particularly refreshing served over ice, an easy to acquire taste with relatively benign effects appreciated by both sexes. The previous learnt association of past generations is fading and it is no wonder that major brewers and alcoholic beverage producers are increasingly looking at this product as a source of potential opportunity and growth.

Indeed, provided the entry problems of the previous UK generation can be avoided and perhaps the acidic astringency reduced, there seems little reason why cider cannot be a major success internationally, particularly in both traditional and the emerging markets where there is no or little cider-drinking history.

Chapter Six

The Encounter

Summary

- **New food and drink experiences are usually obtained through a form of introduction**

- **The what, who, when and how of the introduction are very influential in forming an emotional attachment**

- **Most (but not all) of these introductions occur when growing up**

- **The ideal for such experiences is 80% familiar and 20% new**

- **Managing the consumer's Encounter is crucial for a brand owner**

How, when, where and with whom are all crucial components in forming the conscious and unconscious emotions at the first meeting of any new experience. In life, any new experience, such as a new food and drink, is met with a form of introduction. This is often heavily influenced by the experiences and thoughts of the introducer, be it parent, sibling or friend.

New brands can be met any time in life; however, most (but not all) new flavors are met when growing up. Therefore, every new food or drink a child encounters comes with its own description, tonality or even health warning, from the attitude and behavior of those doing the introduction.

However, the circumstances of the Encounter are also crucial as the child learns that people's emotions, behavior and attitudes are not always consistent and do not always tie in with the actual experience. A mother may say something is nice when it is not. A food served at breakfast time is not a treat but to be compared and categorized against other breakfast foods by the child. The weather and time of year have an influence – hot oatmeal in winter for example. The occasion will also have an impact – a party or something more mundane. A child learns to depend on these environmental cues as much as any cajoling from an introducer – a bullying brother or a kind uncle. The introducer's beliefs, behavior and motivation are all analyzed and stored.

Where it is being introduced is also very influential. Is it in a smart formal place or a casual laid-back venue – an expensive restaurant or a corner diner or café? Is the place exotic, a sunny beach or a bustling city? What have I heard about such places and similar foods in the past? How can the experience be anticipated – exciting or dull?

It is obvious that at the moment of the Encounter many more questions are being posed than in subsequent experiences of the food or drink. Once the product has been seen, classified and categorized no more questions are asked otherwise similar effort would have to be spent on every occasion. Rather, the emotional and intellectual effort at the Encounter is substantial and exhaustive which leads to an inflexible opinion – that is what makes it of such importance to brand owners.

New experiences generally create a strong impression on the human being – both exciting and requiring care in evaluation. Its 'newness' is evaluated and classified against other similar experiences. It can be exciting, dangerous or adventurous but the individual knows instinctively that the experience will not be as intense when repeated subsequently. However, new experiences can be potentially dangerous, or even worse, embarrassing! The ideal for the individual is 80% familiar and 20% new. If the new element is seen as potentially too high, such as constructing DIY flat-packs or learning a new computer program, the individual will be put off and may withdraw from the challenge altogether and reject the experience.

However, once a child moves into its teenage years new experiences become more attractive and experimentation is high, particularly with their accompanying peer group. In old age the willingness to experiment can be diminished, rather routine and familiar patterns are appreciated. New experiences can become a threat and rejected – 'not for me'.

If we look at candy or sweets, it serves as an excellent example of how the Encounter, even in early life, can potentially form life-lasting behavior.

Candy is a sweet, easily-managed treat which appeals to children worldwide. When they are young it is rationed by parents as a bribe for good behavior but under the threat that it is not 'good for your teeth'! However, grandparents shower the child with candy to 'buy' their affection, so mixed messages are projected at the child – but they know they like it and it also has the aura of forbidden fruit which makes it even more attractive!

When the child obtains its first disposable income – allowance money at usually six to seven years old – it immediately uses its new-found financial freedom to buy candy, usually around school. They see their friends and peers also buying candy and often like what they buy – so swap and share.

In school they get bored and need a mood change and use candy as a small treat to relieve the tedium, improve their mood and help concentration. As a teenager, they will move from childish things and seek new experiences; chocolate now becomes a favorite and candy is left behind. However, when they become an adult, on leaving home for college or their first job, they become bored and seek a mood change to help improve their focus and attention. Surprise, surprise, they often revert back to an early sweet treat and comforter from their childhood – candy. To their astonishment they also see that their peer group follows the same behavior and therefore share candy with their fellow co-workers.

It is noticeable that in many offices around the globe jars of candy are frequently on display where workers can share their candy and help themselves when required to stimulate the required mood change – reverting back to the child within and therefore demonstrating the emotional power of the Encounter.

Managing the Encounter

It can be seen, therefore, that managing the Encounter for the appropriate consumer target market is crucial for the brand owner. Is it more appropriate at a smart stylish venue or a local filling station or the local supermarket? For example, new alcoholic drinks are frequently introduced into a limited number of stylish bars to reach opinion formers in the hope their influence will percolate to others. Consumers observe those who are purchasing and often emulate their behavior as it gives an indication of the brand and whether it will support their self-image and value structure – or not!

If it is a food the consumer will go further. They are unlikely to study the ingredient list – despite government and manufacturers cajoling –but they will look at pictures and colors to classify major ingredients. Product shots are very useful to give an indication of what it might be like to eat and whether appropriate for a particular Need State. It therefore needs to be obvious, familiar but exciting which can be difficult for a new product launch. This is one of the reasons why a range extension of a successful brand can be a safer option for the brand owner as long as this has the '80/20 familiarity versus new' connect. If not, there is a danger of damaging the parent brand – either being too close causing cannibalization or too distant and therefore lacking heritage and congruency.

It is obvious that managing the Encounter is key to the introduction of a new brand and requires more thought than simply putting on a big display at the end of the grocer's aisle. Care and thought need to be applied as to how exactly the target market will Encounter the new product. The location and its associated environment, timing (even down to time of day) and particularly who introduces the product can all be crucial to success or failure.

Example of how a Product's Emotions and Physiology Deliver

Alcoholic Spirits

The Northern European and New World attitude to drinking spirits is very different from the Latin countries. In the former, there has been a long history of distilling alcohol, particularly from grain. Perhaps it is required to use its warmth in the palate and stomach to combat harsh winters but many countries in the Northern Hemisphere have their own indigenous spirits – both white and brown – which have been exported with immigration to the New World.

Its use is often as a straight 'short' drink consumed by males as an almost macho signal to peers, or with a mixer consumed by both men and women. In Latin countries there are some spirits derived from local grapes but their consumption is not at the same frequency, as alcohol consumption has traditionally been centered on food and this bias still continues, if being evolved over time in the younger generation.

It is noticeable that the Latin culture seems to foster a 'healthier' and more respectful attitude to alcohol consumption, particularly strong spirits, where consumption is mainly sipping, mellowing and relaxing as opposed to heavy consumption. In Spain, for example, young fashionable adults will be served a white or brown spirit in a very generous measure with a mixer. However, a few of such drinks will be sipped slowly over a period of several hours until very late in the night/early morning. Contrast this with the 'short' culture of many other countries.

The young adult of Northern Europe and North America is likely to be introduced to alcohol through beer if male or wine if female, although white spirits with fruit or cola mixers are often the entry point for young women. Males find beer can be bloating after several glasses while young women often find the quality of wine can be dubious in many pubs, bars and nightclubs. Hence they often turn to spirits with mixers which can be a known quantity and its effects managed by the amount of mixer and rate of consumption, although the effects of both are frequently miscalculated by the young.

The entry point to spirits is usually the more neutral white spirits of vodka and white rum, mixed with the soft drink of teenage years, orange, lemonade or cola. This, therefore, is an easily acquired taste which effectively is like drinking an alcoholic soft drink, either in a glass or straight from the bottle in an Alcopops RTD. Easy, accessible, thirst-quenching with an (almost) seemingly benign effect of slight alcoholic buzz and excitement, such drinks are an ideal entry point for young drinkers. It can be almost too easy and accessible and the effects can often be misjudged in the excitement of a big night out, leading to over-indulgence and heavy inebriation.

The young adult learns through experience that these drinks are not as 'easy' as they initially seem and must be treated with some respect, but significantly they are associated with alcoholic fruit juice and are not seen by many young adults as 'real' drinks but 'OK for kids'.

As their palate becomes more mature, white spirits become to be seen as childish, particularly if they associate them with a 'bad experience'. If a teenager or young adult has such a 'bad' experience with a spirit, even if the drink was easy to consume, they will always associate the drink with vomiting, bad behavior, excess drinking and so forth. This subconsciously makes them feel immature and stupid and therefore such emotions are linked to the identified alcoholic drink. Consequently, it is almost impossible to get them to revisit that drink ever again in later life. Tequila in the US and Pernod in Europe seem particularly resonant examples!

Therefore, many young male adults look to move on to more adult male and sophisticated drinks, particularly in the brown spirit arena. However, they still want to cut the more extreme abrasive and harsh notes produced by brown spirits with their favorite mixers. Fruit juice is seen as too juvenile and feminine but cola is 'ideal'. Its carbonation stimulates the senses while its caramel molasses sweetness blends, smoothes and calms the harsher abrasive notes. Therefore, the brown spirit they select **must** mix with cola. Bourbon is ideal as such a spirit drink, blending perfectly with cola and possessed of a modern trendy image through brilliant positioning. Its first encounter may seem a bit daunting with an image of a hard-drinking spirit not for the faint-hearted. However, the first trial – inevitably with cola – is significantly a pleasant surprise. It is not as harsh as anticipated but neither 'too easy' and has to be acquired with some but not significant effort. It is a challenge but not too challenging. The level of cola and spirit measure is used to control the experience.

It is interesting to compare the Bourbon experience with Scotch whisky (blended, not Malt which has an expensive and more sophisticated quality image). Here we have a spirit consumed by the young male adult's father and grandfather – an old man's drink not of today. Not only does Scotch have this poor image, it also does not mix well with cola for the young palate. The strong, abrasive aroma and wheat/malt notes seem to clash with the sweet carbonated cola, canceling out, not complementing, the caramel richness (unlike Bourbon).

Scotch whisky does work well with ginger ale, but again this is not a common mixer drink for the younger generation and therefore the Scotch and ginger ale combination is old-fashioned and largely irrelevant for the younger generation in the West.

In the East, Scotch drinking is a relatively new experience and the spirit does not have the historical baggage of the West. Therefore, young male adults consider the drink trendy and a badge of fashion from the West – in trendy bars in Shanghai, young affluent Chinese have learned to acquire the taste of Scotch with cola – albeit with a high cola to Scotch ratio – buying into the image rather than the initial taste. The emotional kudos of the status and self-image overrides the difficulty of acquiring the taste. It is no wonder that the Scotch whisky industry looks to the East for its future growth.

Chapter Seven

Health and Wellness

Summary

- The growth of Health and Wellness in food and drink started in the 1970s

- Since the movement it has a convoluted and ever-changing history based around the concept of 'you are what you eat'

- Unfortunately, to achieve this a key component of food and drink – its taste – has often been mislaid

- Ethnic foods and different diets have helped taste to re-emerge

- The overall result is that many are looking to lead a balanced lifestyle in relation to their diet

- Functional foods (BFY and GFY) are attempts by brand owners to assist consumers in achieving this balanced approach

The first link between what we consume and our health occurred in the 1950s as well as the link between smoking and cancer, although major changes in behavior did not commence until the 1970s. This was followed by the realization that exercise was good for you and could prevent heart disease – hence the jogging and aerobic classes boom.

The first major link between diet and health was that heart disease was also affected by diet. Salt was the first 'criminal' ingredient. Excessive salt intake was shown to increase blood pressure which can then lead to heart disease. All over the western world sodium intake was reduced, including as a cooking ingredient and any foods containing salt. This was the first round in reducing taste in food!

Next came sugar, initially for its calorific value but also linked to a growth in diabetes. This was followed by some managing of ingredients, such as in Europe the introduction of 'E' numbers to classify and list accepted food additives. Consumers started to examine the ingredient lists on packs from a fear of artificial ingredients – although many soon tired of the effort. Also red meat came under the microscope, particularly the effect of fat. The result of all this examination was the philosophy of 'you are what you eat', so foods with a positive health role, such as fiber, were encouraged, yoghurt became more acceptable and whilst skimmed and semi-skimmed milk was 'OK', full-fat milk, butter and cheese were not. Carbonated soft drinks came under attack for their sugar but the industry counter-attacked with diet drinks containing artificial sweeteners.

The overall result of the dietary changes which largely encompassed the 1970s and 1980s was that society had effectively challenged the major carriers and components of taste, i.e. salt, sugar, fat and dairy products. Many food products and meals tasted poor.

While trial of these 'new' foods was extensive, particularly amongst the middle class, the market began to differentiate and fragment as an individual's tolerance limits were pushed too far and a counteraction occurred. There was (and still is) the belief that if you controlled your diet and exercised you could look younger, fitter, healthier and ultimately extend your life span. However, diversity began to occur and in the US obesity began.

By the 1990s there were those who followed a diet and exercise regime (or tried to) and at the other extreme there were those who rejected such a lifestyle and over-indulged. However, there was such massive pressure to conform, particularly on women, in magazines and other media that it became a firm topic at dinner parties. Visible 'badges' of a healthy lifestyle such as sneakers and sports-orientated casual clothing became popular.

The growth of the working mother also played a role as many of these new foods did not lend themselves to three formal meals a day. Rather, aided by the microwave and new simple ready-meal formats, grazing by all the family and snacking on the go became the norm. However, there was still a need for hunger and taste satisfaction – absent within acceptable norms – and ethnic foods from the East came to the rescue.

Most of the ethnic foods originate from countries where the quality and quantity of meat was low. The result was that high-impact spices and flavors were used to cover the taste of the meat. The high-impact foods satisfied through their intensity rather than their sustenance. Human beings are easily confused between a high-intensity strong taste and a full stomach – they are fooled into thinking that they have eaten more than they actually have. The ethnic foods do contain fat but it is concealed – as is the guilt. Many of the spices are also a good substitute for sweetness. Here is the 'perfect' food: when eaten it gives maximum in-mouth satisfaction and hunger is initially satisfied although this tended to fade. Also because the ingredients were not obvious, most felt they had permission to eat.

Conversely, the equivalent 'ethnic' global export from the USA, fast food, also contains high taste with strong sweetness, but is viewed with suspicion as the ingredients can be easily identified and are very familiar to signal guilt.

The drive for greater health but with taste satisfaction took Northern Europe to the Mediterranean diet based around olive oil, fish, vegetables and a little wine. Here at last was something satisfying with good flavor but was emotionally rewarding as it was blatantly healthy.

Consumers were now looking to retain some adult perspective after the first health obsessions and were looking for a balance of health and satisfaction. This meant that they looked at their total diet, allowing themselves some limited indulgence if it had been 'earned' by 'being good' through other healthy eating. This can be a couple of days before an indulgence is allowed and as a result a meal could become flexible – even stretching over a few days. The absence of calories from Tuesday could be enjoyed on Friday evening, even as a fast food meal. Flexibility of food and food consumption occasion fitted into our grazing and snacking habits perfectly.

Functional Foods

As life spans have increased so too has the interest in taking care of oneself, fueled by the growth of baby boomers into middle and older age. Medical science preaches that all things are possible; consumers are therefore prepared to invest in anything that might extend their enjoyment and life expectancy. They do realize that no one magic food or ingredient will accomplish this, but that a whole raft of initiatives could potentially make this probable or at least possible – hence the growth in functional foods.

At the same time the drug culture has impacted on the younger generation's attitude to food and drink. For example, the learning that a certain colored pill produces a certain effect and state of mind also extends to alcoholic drinks where different drinks will produce different states and levels of inebriation. So today's younger adults and late teens now see nearly all foods in a categorizing sense – they are good or bad, they produce X or Y response physiologically and deliver varied and different rewards. This makes the idea of functional foods very credible, despite the efforts of regulatory bodies to limit the claims made for such foods. As long as brand owners deliver these benefits in foods which do not cause the consumer to question its validity though wrong emotional messages of taste and texture, the consumer will find it appealing. Overstep the mark – a 'healthy' hamburger strains credibility or 'cream cakes are good for you' – and the consumer's learnt values of healthy eating will come into play.

The consumer is, therefore, reacting intellectually and emotionally to foods consumed and their quantity and making a conscious decision based on how they feel eating it to match a recognized ideal. Many young girls now judge a food by how it feels in the stomach, for example, and will reject those foods that feel heavy or cause bloating in the stomach. Effectively they are training themselves to be hungry. Whilst it is easy to blame emaciated models for enforcing this culture, the reality is driven by inner feelings of consumption that reinforce the emotions that drive self-image.

We have, therefore, a society in which people are more conscious of how their body feels than previous generations. The baby boomer bulge is carrying that through the age cohorts, realizing that there is a direct connection between diet, exercise, quality of life and how these aspects relate directly to health and lifespan. The younger generation is reinforcing this trend by judging food by how it feels and their body response. As they have children it is likely that they will pass this on to the next generation. Increasingly, food and drink are being appraised not only by how they taste but also by the impact of texture signals in the mouth and stomach plus other physiological and emotional rewards.

The food and drink brand owners will increasingly design their foods to react to these changing requirements – probably using functional foods with the maximum implied benefit, either through direct claims or through ingredients and/or implied positioning as Good for You (often difficult to prove) and Better for You (easier and more credible to the consumer).

Chapter Eight

Obesity – The Role of Flavor

Summary

- The emotions behind the taste of fast and processed foods can be very powerful and satisfying

- They provide messages of safety, comfort and security as Emotional Support

- People become potentially addicted to these messages, not necessarily to the foods themselves

- The introduction of 'healthier' taste notes in such foods could potentially break this emotional link

Unfortunately, everything we have learned about the psychology of flavors and how they drive emotions positions them directly as a major driving force to greater, not less, consumption.

The key ingredients in both fast foods and processed products are firstly softness in the mouth requires minimal chewing, enabling rapid eating and swallowing of bite-sized portions, largely whole. Sweetness supported by saltiness maximizes both the taste and sugar impact and enhances the flavor delivery. Fats and oils – vegetable, sugar and mineral-based – carry the flavor throughout the mouth, maximizing the number of taste receptors involved, so enhancing the flavor duration and hence, awareness. They are also both volatile and reach into the olfactory organ, the nose, creating even further flavor emotional messages and last in the mouth, often for hours. This is one basis for compulsive eating – the leaving of a 'flavor trail' that slowly fades and demands its recapture.

If people had to chew the food to extract the flavor enjoyment it would take longer to eat, be better digested and the feeling of being full reached far sooner. People would need to consume less.

So we can see that these foods are specifically designed to target the greatest and longest flavor satisfaction that is possible and generate compulsive eating even before we consider the messages that the tastes actually create in the consumer's mind.

Governments know processed food is unhealthy but appear to have no idea why it is so popular.

It is worthwhile to examine the flavors and eats themselves. The single most satisfying in-mouth experience is the flowing across the tongue of a rich syrup or what we refer to as the 'Melt' which is explained in detail later in the book. This slows the heart rate, relaxes the consumer and creates a mellow disposition. It reduces stress. As a party or family shares this food such as pizza so the stress reduction creates bonding, unity of purpose and shared pleasure. It is similar to that of a family eating together but better, far better, even than a true feast. There are no portion or fairness problems, everyone's meal is equal and the delight shared out evenly. Because these savory meals appear to be real food, not confectionery or snacks, the absence of guilt encourages the frequency of these events. The actual flavors themselves are related to those homely notes that recall in the unconscious mind the arrival home from school in childhood, the shared family eating events and the comfort of soups, soft savories, buttered toast and desserts.

Fast food can make you feel safe! Processed food can make you feel family protection and secure! This potentially safe and secure food has the potential to damage your health. The harder your life, and the fewer pleasures it delivers, the more processed foods help you to feel better. It seems similar to alcohol and cigarettes, as a delivery vehicle for pleasure relief or simply escape; what is more, it works. It is too easy for those without the stresses of an unsatisfactory or difficult life to critique others for consuming such foods and becoming obese, in much the same way as non-smokers or non-drinkers are baffled why anybody should smoke or drink (reformed smokers and drinkers have even stronger feelings!).

The answer lies in changing the foods, breaking the messages of comfort and hope. It is largely a waste of time and effort trying to persuade people to eat fruit and vegetables since unless you have associated these from childhood with Family and Security of Home they cannot deliver the emotional needs that processed foods can. People can understand cognitively what the right diet should be, but unless that delivers the 'Emotional Support' of processed foods it requires too great an emotive loss to give up these tastes and mouthfeels. It is here that the addiction lies.

People are addicted to how these foods make them feel, not to the foods themselves. We have done research work on alcohol products, smoking and indeed both pharmaceutical and recreational drugs, for over thirty years, all over the world – and it is the same everywhere. Obesity follows the arrival of processed foods with an absolutely pure correlation. With these items reaching the emerging markets, as food costs rise it is absolutely certain that not only will there be an exploding population but that population will individually be exploding too!

People draw emotional comfort from their food. This is largely based on their positive childhood learnt experiences. In previous generations these were built around 'home-made' dishes where the ingredients were more controlled – often based on availability. Newer, more convenient, exciting and flavorsome processed foods have superseded in many cases the home-made versions. However, these processed foods are more addictive and of less nutritional substance.

How does this slide to Obesity occur?

The findings of our work show that obesity, like alcohol and to an extent drugs, runs in families. There does appear to be a propensity to habitual or addictive behavior with certain people. If they gain emotional benefit from an activity, they tend to over-indulge in that pastime. Others balance their pleasures more carefully.

Income and the expectancy of others whose acceptance is sought is another powerful influence. You behave as those do around you. So as you go down the social scale and the choice of pleasures can be harder to acquire, so you gravitate to those you can afford. This means the cheapest addictions and therefore, less obviously, 'wrong' food is one of the less guilty attractions. That is where you find the greatest problem. It is patronizing to see this as ignorance or weak-willed; it is merely the cheapest solution. One has to eat anyway, so the food is the cheapest option. A consequence is that overweight parents tend to have similar children.

So the obvious question is how is the habit formed amongst people whose parents are in the normal weight range?

Tastes are first experienced and are compared to already known flavors and experiences. 'This tastes a bit like X' or 'the texture is very like Y'. Humans, in order to cope with complexity and ease of recall, make conclusions about experiences, often talking them over with others. This enables a shorthand view composed of a very few words to be logged in the brain as their opinion of that experience. 'Holidays are great'; 'Tax is annoying but necessary'; 'I like cold beer'.

This series of categorized ideas become concepts and tend to remain fixed unless serious new evidence is experienced. You could describe these as a 'branding' of the activity or experience. This enables us to handle the complexity of modern life; we do not need to think through how we feel about everything every time we experience it. Furthermore, most of these categories are emotional preferences justified by a flawed logic. We hold views that suit our personality not those that our brain has deduced.

So attempts to persuade people to change behavior by appealing to their cognitive skills are only effective when the individual is desperate and prepared to review their opinion seriously. In food terms, I give up sugar in coffee only when being very serious about sugar intake and six weeks later – and it does take six weeks – I cannot stand sweet coffee. We then reclassify coffee and we start to reduce the sweetness level in all our other foods. Now we have become a person who does not like sweet things and look down on those who do with great emotional smugness.

Since those who have made an active choice to refrain from fast and processed foods have had to give up some indulgence that they really liked, so they now have no patience for those that have not done so. It is dogmatic fervor of the worst kind. Yet that key consumption change was not merely symbolic but, more significantly, it was the catalyst of the change for them.

How to Change Behavior

The acquisition by the consumer of an active preference for fast food tastes, flavors and mouthfeel occurs because the fun and informal nature of fast food consumption, when people first experience it, is extraordinarily attractive. It is far more fun than normal food at home. Take any child out for a meal and they just adore the event –happy faces all around, laughter and the maximum of family harmony. It is an event that cries out to be repeated; hence the demand for children's parties at McDonalds, Pizza Hut, etc.

This is the best social event in a pre-teen's normal life and what gets the credit? It is the location and the food itself. So, every time fast food is suggested the child recalls the happiness, lack of formality and the freedom of fast food. The flavor is noted equally, but this time unconsciously triggers the same emotional response. Taste McDonalds and you are 'eating freedom'. So it is addictive, flavor and mouthfeel too. Now whenever those flavor notes occur in other processed foods they create this conditioned, but unaware, response. They are immediately liked and the person feels good! That is at the heart of the constant over-eating amongst today's youth. Until you break that response you will never change that 'learned palate'.

Can governments influence this? It is very difficult to enforce and needs a complete revaluation and rethink of both food and health behavior. However, forcing this on consumers would undoubtedly produce a negative reaction. The introduction of healthier notes in processed fast food over a period of years could potentially alter the conscious and subconscious emotions linking processed foods with 'unhealthy' tastes. Therefore, grains, pulses, vegetable and fruit flavors are perceived as being part of delivering of the desired emotional fulfillment. We could explore this further but probably in another book!

Chapter Nine

The Influence of Culture

Summary

- **Historically, climate and geography create the foods that are the basis of a country's diet**

- **The growth of international trade and expansion led to importing of diverse foods and spices to liven the diet**

- **The style of the family culture and the method of eating is a large determiner of the taste palate**

- **However, some specific foods have an appeal that transcends culture and country**

If we look at different cultures we inevitably see the role of climate and geography and its impact and influence in creating indigenous foods as the basis of local diet. These foods are often available and cheap.

Historically, the quality of water was dubious particularly in North European countries. The safest way to kill off the bugs was to turn it into alcohol which gave a good measure of taste and refreshment along with a merry kick! In warmer Mediterranean climates, vines flourished and wine became the preferred option, while in the colder Northern Europe beer emerged.

When some of the people of Europe later migrated they took their preferred alcoholic choice with them to the New Worlds of USA, Australia, Canada, New Zealand and South Africa. These were in turn altered by the local climate and available ingredients to form their own individual tastes.

In food, salting was used heavily in northern countries to extend the shelf life of meat and fish, as was smoking to produce heavily individualistic strong tastes and preferences. In addition, the soil and climate made a huge difference to the fruit, vegetables and cereals grown. In the Mediterranean, farming tends to be small, localized and enough for small families, leading to a surprisingly localized diet, while in North America the enormous wheat and corn fields of the Midwest have produced breakfast cereals and grain-fed cattle.

The UK, Holland, Belgium and other European countries imported interesting foods and spices from their empires to impact and enrich what many consider a bland diet. These foods and flavors were combined to form adulterated dishes such as Chicken Masala in the UK to suit local tastes and ingredients.

Other cultural influences which impact on diet, and therefore the learning of an adult taste palate, are the style of family structure and eating. These are often driven by custom, local conditions and religious beliefs, the food reflecting the society.

In these cultures where the family is at the top of the priority list, children tend to be highly valued and more involved in adult interaction. This includes making an occasion of the family dinner, when all direct and often extended members of the family 'break bread' together.

In Southern Europe and parts of Asia this is the major consumption occasion of the day, with the head of the household holding court and demonstrating attitudes and behavior to the children about food and drink – including table manners. One result of this in Southern Europe is a huge respect for food and rituals associated with food, across many varied courses and dishes. Even small children join the meal and eat a toned-down version of the dishes; older children are encouraged to drink diluted wine and coffee. This leads to a much healthier appreciation of both drinks in later life – much less of a case of consuming forbidden fruit than in other cultures.

In those cultures where individual freedom is highly valued and the family unit plays a lesser role, this has an inevitable impact on food and drink consumption. Taking parts of Scandinavia and Northern Europe as an example, children are given substantial freedom, justified by social agreements.

The result is more broken families, higher divorce rate and, in food terms, substantial grazing and snacking. Food is often consumed individually on the run, at different times of the day, often by hand and standing up. Foods are taken out of the fridge and microwaved for convenience; pizza, burgers and nuggets are consumed by children without a knife and fork – so that some children do not know how to use cutlery properly or eat with manners when teenagers.

We can see that culture is a major determiner of the taste palate. However, certain tastes and textures seem to transcend culture and have almost universal appeal no matter from where they originated.

For example, bacon and eggs, chili con carne, pizza and pasta in various formats, sweet and sour pork, steak and chips, hamburgers and, of course, cola to name but a few, plus dishes from China, India and Thailand.

The key to the appeal of such foods is based around taste and texture contrasts. They have soft and hard components, sometimes a crisp and chewy element. All the great foods provide textural stimulus at the front of the mouth and also a contrast at the rear of mouth on which to chew to prolong the satisfaction. For taste terms they initially are sharp, intrusive and impact at the front of the mouth with rich, heavier, slower tastes that relax you in the rear of the mouth. Sweetness is also present along with fat to carry the flavor, through caramelization in the cooking process by adding specific additional ingredients.

This type of food often transcends different occasions and is so enjoyed that it is often force-fitted into an occasion for which it is not designed; the food and drink is so good, so enjoyable, stimulating and rewarding.

In contemporary terms, some branded food items which start in one consumption occasion gravitate to another simply because the consumer loves them so much. It may start out as party food, full of life and excitement, but is so delicious that it ends up being eaten alone in front of the TV. Ice cream, chips and chocolate are all examples.

Example of how a Product's Emotions and Physiology Deliver

Coffee

In many countries coffee is seen as a powerful adult drink with a significant caffeine kick which needs to be treated with respect. It becomes part of the adult 'rite of passage' with many consumers' first encounter coming later in life than their first experience of alcohol. Children in such cultures rarely try coffee until in their late teens or early 20s – it is seen as too harsh and powerful a taste for anybody younger. It is not until they go to college or start their first job that they try coffee. They are now in an 'adult' world which requires a higher level of preparedness and concentration for the tasks ahead and coffee is often the drink of choice of their peers, so they adopt and copy their environment's choice.

Coffee's inherent taste is bitter and difficult to acquire, so they manage the challenge with milk, cream and sugar to smooth out the more powerful notes to deliver an acceptable taste. As their palate matures they learn to manage that taste – possibly consuming stronger coffee as they get older or even giving up milk, cream or sugar for health reasons. It normally takes up to six weeks to bear to cut out sugar from coffee; however, once that taste is learnt it is almost impossible to go back to the former sweetness level. The individual learns to adjust and acquire the taste that fits their circumstances and preference.

However, coffee is still a powerful drink which is both a stimulant and relaxant with an easy kick accompanied by soothing refreshment. These powerful physiological and emotional messages deliver similar values to alcohol and chocolate – products which deliver conscious and subconscious emotions at a high level. Coffee therefore has similar properties; the bitterness in the rear mouth and aftertaste is often thought to represent the caffeine kick – no bitterness, no kick. This is untrue but a commonly-held perception of coffee's power and kick.

The other area which demonstrates the emotional power of coffee is the ritual which is often used to prepare and serve fresh coffee. The granules are often ground from fresh beans and must be just the 'right' amount in proportion to the water to be used. Many consumers have a favorite coffee pot or coffee-making machine, the taste of the coffee it produces is unlike any other and cannot ever be replicated by another machine (allegedly!).

The coffee is served in a favorite cup with any required cream, milk or sugar. It is seemingly impossible to start the day without the coffee and its associated ritual; failure to do so can potentially ruin the whole day. Such is the physiological and emotional appeal of coffee. In countries where instant coffee dominates it still has a powerful emotional meaning but accompanied by less ritual.

It is interesting to note that many older generation consumers in the US find Starbucks' coffee too strong and bitter. Younger consumers in the US seem to have acquired the taste even if the beverage is mostly diluted in a milky cappuccino or latte format.

However, in many countries, particularly those with a Latin, Mediterranean or South American culture, the attitude to coffee is very different. It is often the beverage of choice for the household with a ready, fresh pot 'on the stove' all day. Children are exposed to its taste from an early age, but heavily diluted with milk and sugar. In such cultures (as with wine which is often served diluted to children), the attitude to coffee is of familiarity and healthy respect.

The result is that they drink stronger coffee more frequently and start at a younger age – without any seeming adverse side effects. In the US, with the growing influence of immigrants from such countries plus the effect of the younger consumer's palate preferring more intense tastes, helped by Starbucks, it would be surprising if the coffee palate of the US did not change to more and stronger coffee in the day. The bulk of present day coffee drinking in the US, often two cups, even one in the morning with a possible exception of a cup after a meal event, is the norm. The beverage still has that powerful image which means it must be handled with care to avoid being 'too wired'. This is directly opposite to the growing Latin and emerging US younger palate.

Chapter Ten

Taste Globalization

Summary

- **The youth of the world are moving closer together in diet**

- **This provides a huge opportunity for international food and drink brands in areas such as the BRIC markets**

- **However, mitigating against this is the learnt taste palate of such markets which varies considerably**

- **The key is to understand the market and modify the brand according to the local palate – not rely on trial and error**

Increasingly we live in a global village with instant communication and more convenient and swift travel to even the most exotic and far-flung destinations. This has led to a more homogenous planet with the skyline of big city architecture conforming to the same patterns so that the international traveler seems at home on most continents.

This conformity of lifestyle also reaches to human behavior with the citizens of global cities traveling on the same transport systems to the same type of work in similar surroundings, shopping at the same malls and all eating the same food. Or is the last statement correct? Has the global taste palate arrived along with other forms of globalization?

Undoubtedly there has been a drawing together of different lifestyles including in food and drink. This has applied particularly to the younger generation with Parisian youngsters enjoying American fast food to the annoyance of their elders.

In the West we have also increasingly enjoyed the benefits of 'ethnic' food particularly from the East.

What is particularly interesting is that the youth of Europe, the US and Australasia are moving closer and closer in dietary terms.

In Italy more beer is consumed by teenagers than wine. The Spanish mix Coca-Cola with their indigenous alcoholic drinks. The hamburger has moved across Europe and products such as coffee are treated with great respect and handled carefully by young Europeans. Coffee can be regarded as more dangerous than many alcoholic drinks for older teenagers. Even in an established market such as the US, taste preference amongst the young is moving towards a more intense palate driven by high-impact fast food and soft drinks coupled with growing spicy ethnic food.

The teen generation watches the same films, they wear the same clothes, listen to the same music, follow the same celebrities and use the same social media formats. They are the first globalized taste palate generation. They share more in common with their age cohorts three thousand miles away than they do in dietary terms with their parents in their very own home!

This will provide a revolution and a huge opportunity for brands to develop and extend worldwide. These brands will find high and positive responses should they get the recipe, the taste, the texture and the eating experience right. Winning a global race to match the emerging worldwide palate will reap unprecedented rewards. Many of today's monster brands will not make it; they were created in a different age for a different palate and consumption occasion. They deliver emotions that are all less and less relevant today.

It is the major developing markets such as Brazil, China, India and Russia (BRIC) which increasingly attract the attention of the international food and beverage giants compared with their relatively static or even declining traditional western markets. These new developing markets – and the Far East in general – offer enormous potential for future growth to the international food and beverage companies with their global brands. However, it is interesting to see what problems these global companies are facing in penetrating these developing markets.

In China, for example, some of the western fast food chains are having limited success as, although the environment is liked, some of the foods are not, while ice cream and coffee are achieving low penetration. Just ask anybody expecting a coffee at a business meeting only to receive the traditional lukewarm water if coffee is doing well!

Starbucks is making strenuous efforts to expand in China but has less than 400 mainland outlets compared to nearly 900 in Japan. These Chinese outlets are mainly concentrated on the Eastern Seaboard cities where the population seems to have bought into the Starbucks 'café' experience rather than the coffee itself – although the likelihood is that Starbucks will grow if they follow their Japanese model of offering local tea variations.

Intense, rich, dairy fatty flavors are an anathema in China so ice cream struggles while bitterness combined with a slight sourness is appreciated in many foods. Contrast this with India where creaminess is appreciated in ice cream and desserts, the opposite of its neighbor, while creaminess is Russia is more associated with a slight sour acidity from yogurt and sour cream rather than full, rich creaminess or even its opposite, fruity acidity.

The converse can be applied to popular western 'ethnic' foods; most native Chinese or Indians would struggle with the westernized interpretation because of flavor modifications of their classic cuisine dishes. Therefore we cannot say that globalization has occurred in the taste palate.

The question arises for the international food and beverage marketer: why is this fact seemingly so apparent in some categories compared to others?

The key to understanding the global palate is to realize, as previously stated, that taste is a learnt experience, largely but not exclusively derived from our childhood, developed as a teenager and matured as an adult. New foods when encountered are evaluated, even at a subconscious level, to previous experiences of similar foods eaten on similar occasions. Preference is, after all, based on positive emotions previously encountered. A Szechuan Chinese man encountering a bland fish dish will evaluate the experience not only against other fish dishes but also against his lifetime experience of eating chili as a major food ingredient and will therefore reject the dish accordingly.

How can the large international food and beverage companies tap into and influence such a palate based on a lifetime's experience? The key is to understand the local taste palate of a market plus, importantly, the emotions that are being generated by similar foods in meeting the requirements of the consumer's target Need State (the motivation for the consumption occasion). Often minor tweaks which take account of the local taste palate can have dramatic effects on manipulating the product consumption to fulfill the consumer's desired emotional satisfaction. The overall objective is to make the product more appropriate to the local psychological and physiological needs – and not rely on 20 years' presence of persisting with the same taste profile as trial and error to change a nation; it will not.

A product designed for the West Coast of America will not automatically succeed on the East Coast of China. The successful large international food and beverage companies learn this lesson and those that do not will struggle to enforce global models of taste delivery on individual market taste preference.

Today, however, some globalization of the palate amongst today's teens is definitely emerging, as previously discussed. That globalization affects Europe, the US and Australasia, but less so Asia or Africa. Asia is more flavor and ingredient aware than the West, but is interestingly less comfortable with emotional response to stimuli.

The multinationals are not powerless. They do not have to pursue slavishly the different countries' palates. It is possible to influence the taste palate. Big corporations should see their brand portfolios not as meeting a series of disconnected needs but more as a process of educating the palate and communicating the beliefs triggered by the different brands' tastes and mouthfeels. It is perfectly possible to market a children's product that will predispose the child to prefer certain flavors in their teens. This can then be structured so that the taste characteristics owned by the company's brands have a linkage through a lifetime. The brands are then acting synergistically to educate the broader construction of the taste palate in the direction of their choice.

Therefore the brand owner who does not understand the delivery, in eating and drinking terms, of all their brands and how this fits or does not fit with the taste palates (its values and emotions) is flying blind and without radar.

The palate is constantly moving and evolving. People seek new experiences in taste as in life and can become fussier as they improve their quality of life. Today's popular flavor combination can be an anachronism in ten short years' time. The result is that the brand can die with it.

PART TWO

Chapter Eleven

The Journey of Taste

Summary

- **All food and drink products undergo a complex Journey of Taste which consists of a number of interrelated stages**

- **These stages must work in harmony to produce the desired emotional response successfully**

- **The stages consist of Appearance, Aroma, Front of Mouth, Mid and Rear Mouth, Aftertaste and After-Effects**

- **Appearance – taste is often anticipated from visual cues**

- **Aroma – must fit in with the other components of the journey**

- **Front of Mouth – potentially forms the initial judgment which is often associated with stimulation and excitement**

- **Mid and Rear Mouth – where more complex messages emerge**

- **Aftertaste and After-Effects – critical to the enjoyment of the product and whether it is revisited (or not!)**

All food and drink products undergo a Journey of Taste in their consumption experience. The journey has a start, middle and end before being repeated in the next portion or gulp. If this journey provides the emotional satisfaction that is required by the consumer to fulfill the targeted Need State, then that journey will be categorized as suitable and attractive and, therefore, likely to be repeated. If it fails to deliver, the product will be rejected and alternatives will be examined until preference occurs.

This may sound simple but the reality is quite complex and features a series of interrelated stages in the journey. Commencing with the appearance and aroma, it moves to the initial front of mouth hit, flows into the mid mouth, then to the rear mouth and then is swallowed to be realized in the aftertaste and sometimes after-effects in the stomach. Throughout this journey, complex and varied tastes are potentially being released through texture and mouthfeel which reflect the nature and consistency of the product being consumed.

In order for the desired emotions to provide consumer preference and satisfaction this depends on the internalization of all the functions working in harmony. If one aspect of the Journey of Taste is out of alignment then the product is subject to severe questioning and probable rejection. For a brand owner to succeed it is vital that the Journey of Taste is understood and optimized to realize the desired consumer emotional preference. Failure leads to losing competitive advantage to those companies who provide a better experience and consequent falling sales. The global marketplace is littered with such examples.

To avoid such pain it is necessary to go through the individual aspects of the Journey of Taste in a structured approach and illustrate their importance.

Appearance

In most instances, the first element of the Journey of Taste is the visual appearance. Consumers are usually very good at diagnosing the likely consumption experiences from the appearance of a food or drink. They will usually interpret the specific ingredients, textures and likely balance of the ingredients' flavor impact, anticipating the whole product's taste not just separate flavors. To demonstrate these cues, let's examine a number of different product types as examples – cakes, savory pies and meat, chocolate confectionery and beverages.

A cake enthusiast will examine the number of layers, the fruit, cream, jam/jelly, judge the likely weight and texture plus the contribution from the flavor and texture of different cake types, shades and fillings – cheesecake versus a gateau. They will judge the likely weight in the mouth, how firm, soft, chewy or delicate – they want to see the whole mixture of tastes and visualize the idea of a full bite.

Color is also very important in providing visual cues. Is it bright, with contrast, a 'fresh' color to give the consumer an idea about flavor? Darker cake means richer, heavier with a greater sugar, dried fruit or syrup content. A lighter color means possible lighter texture and a lighter, possible sponge eat. The density and depth of filling will suggest confirmation of lightness or richness. The color attracts and gives indications as to where the main tastes will originate.

Red suggests berry or cherry, sour fruit or sweet while darker colors suggest the richness of chocolate, coffee, alcohol or nuts. This helps in the psychology of the Need State; is it a colorful celebration and extrovert or packed with heavy, rich ingredients which suggest relaxation and contentment?

With heavier savory items, focus is placed on the balance of ingredients, particularly cooked meats, its size and quality, its leanness and fat content. The likely animal and possibly the original cut are all considered plus the color fitting the ingredients.

Components that accompany the meat are also visually examined, whether pasta, vegetable, bread or pastry, for their balance, preparation and fit with the meat. For products that have pastry which is cooked such as sweet pies or similar, the shape needs to show a generosity and fullness, an almost crafted element in a mass-produced product. A color that reflects the different shades of baking, cooking and grilling plus contoured highs and lows from the rising of the pastry in that cooking process is valued. Flat and uniform is viewed with suspicion.

With chocolate confectionery there is a great deal of emotional fulfillment generated by the consumption – hence the appearance will help in the anticipation of that fulfillment. The consumer has an almost X-ray ability to judge the quality and thickness of the chocolate in a chocolate biscuit or countline, say a Kit Kat. The shape and corners of the bar or piece of chocolate give an indication of the depth of chocolate. This directly signals the level of quality, indulgence and weight of the eat, the likely size of the product's interior filling or if solid chocolate, how and why it will be eaten and the appropriate form of occasion or anticipated Need State.

If the bar is seen as substantial it is likely to be seen as fuel, filling and providing energy as a possible meal substitute. However, if visually it looks lighter, livelier, snappy and texturally crisp and/or crunchy then the expectation is something which will provide stimulation and a break or change in mind and mood. This is ideal for a short stimulating snack which will not satiate or be too rich and will be ideal with a hot or cold drink.

The appearance of solid chocolate in a bar is crucial. The depth of chocolate color indicates creamy richness, or if dark then possible cocoa bitterness. The size and shape of the individual chunks and pieces of the bar are very significant. In the mind of the consumer, particularly females, this will set the ritual, time and location of consumption. It will determine whether the product is likely to be bitten, licked, nibbled, sucked or chewed or the likely combination to obtain the maximum satisfaction from the eat. The depth, size and smoothness of the edge contributes heavily to the style of eat, whether shared in company or eaten on one's own.

Many women like to bite a chunk or piece of solid chocolate in half, play with the little chunk in the mouth, allowing it to melt before placing the piece against the roof of the mouth until it dissolves before swallowing – a process that can take up to several minutes. If the visual shape of the chocolate chunk or piece is too jagged, sharp or seemingly largely hard and intrusive then the chocolate will be rejected or used and eaten in another Need State.

With many alcoholic drinks the color is a strong indicator of taste; generally the darker the color, the more intense the taste. In beer, it is the carbonation and the head when served on draught. The head subconsciously smoothes and softens the taste hit and carries the taste through the mouth in a slower and reflective manner. In addition, for brown spirits, wine and beer the depth and intensity of color indicates complexity and weight of taste – Guinness versus Budweiser for example.

In soft drinks the color is far more likely to drive the consumer directly to a flavor area such as fruit variant. So, for example, the intensity of an orange color in a drink will indicate the level of acidity and possible refreshment. Pulp or creaminess in an orange drink indicates less refreshment but more hedonistic satisfaction.

Visual examination is largely rational, deductive and conscious but it can stir unconscious emotional responses which have been previously categorized, making it an important component in the Journey of Taste. Many consumers find it easier to describe the likely taste experience prior to consumption from the visual appearance as opposed to describing the taste experience after the product is eaten. No wonder that the product's appearance on packaging is so important in setting up the experience. It is easy to anticipate the taste from visual cues at the start of the Journey of Taste.

Aroma

Following the initial appearance, the consumer makes judgments based on the aroma generated by a product but not to the same extent as appearance. In most cases the initial top notes serve as a guide, particularly for freshness or otherwise; if any 'off' notes occur, this immediately raises suspicions as to the suitability of the product at an instinctive level.

Attractive aromas can trigger the appetite and produce saliva based on learnt experience and emotions. Food retailers will often circulate the aroma of freshly-baked bread, fresh ground coffee or even grilled meat around their store to attract the shopper by an almost Pavlovian response.

Consumers instinctively know that the aroma of freshly-brewed coffee will not be matched by the taste. However, they do desire emotional satisfaction from the warm, evocative and relaxing aroma notes to generate familiar relaxation which continues to be appreciated throughout the drink – a vital part of the coffee consumption process and ritual. However, apart from a few critical instances such as those mentioned above, the consumer will not attach much importance to the aroma, as by and large it will not assist in ascertaining whether the product is sweet, salty, sour or bitter. Smell is not a finely-developed sense; even though scientists acknowledge that most tastes are generated by the nose, the consumer does not make the link and relies more on the taste.

The nose tends to be a better judge of the cooking process rather than the ingredients. However, frying food can signal guilt through its unhealthy, heavy and sticky aroma to those with a healthy eating outlook versus those who love fried bacon! It depends on your eating strategy and emotional beliefs tied to different occasions. The cooking aroma can be a major source in helping the consumer place and position the food. They may be familiar with those notes and therefore they can trigger association and location – BBQs outside on a summer day or a family occasion such as Christmas or Thanksgiving.

The aroma can therefore set the scene for the Consumption Experience and transport the consumer into a pre-defined set of moods and emotions: safety, trustworthy, exciting, celebration or the formality of the occasion – casual or formal – fast food or fine dining.

When the aroma is strange or unfamiliar it can be seen as artificial or 'not real' and treated with suspicion, particularly when the visual appearance does not synergistically fit with the aroma, and the product is often rejected. This is because the consumer will often judge how much of a food they will eat based on the confirmed aroma and appearance: 'this sauce is very rich' or 'too many French fries' or 'a light snack' and so forth.

If in turn the brand owner has produced a product which does not match the expectation, then dissonance occurs. The cues did not match the taste and texture, too much sweetness, fat or weight. Every time the consumer is worried by such an experience, it increases the likelihood of not finishing the product – they feel that they have been directionally misled and fooled.

The aroma must 'fit' with the other components of the Journey of Taste for a product otherwise it is a poor emotional fit for the consumer.

Front of Mouth

The first impact from the front of mouth can formulate the initial taste and texture judgment in the Journey of Taste.

The front of mouth is associated with stimulation and initial excitement from both taste and texture. The crumbliness or crunchiness of the first bite allied to a good impactful taste hit can be very powerful. It can change the mood by working on the brain and change thought patterns into an active and positive framework, particularly when delivering a sharp, clean, light and fresh taste hit. The tone for the whole remaining Journey of Taste is set by this first impression.

Sweetness is usually a crucial part of this impact. Flavors that have inherent sweetness or the sweetness element of a complex food will first be detected at the front of mouth.

In this process, the mind is already consciously and unconsciously sorting out the message from taste and texture. Is it recognizable? Does it fit with the situation I am in now? Do I approve of the flavor or reject it?

Mid and Rear Mouth

As the product moves back through the mouth into the pit and sides of the tongue, then more complex messages start to emerge which can alter initial judgment about the food and cause re-evaluation.

These tastes can be brief, if varied; however, these messages may be delayed by temperature, fats and pH so they are first detected at the front of the mouth, where more complex tastes are savored and deeper emotions are generated before moving into the rear mouth.

Flavors in these areas tend to be the richer, slower, more indulgent, calming and relaxing, taking the consumer into contemplation and satisfaction if delivered correctly, setting up the crucial area of the aftertaste.

Aftertaste and After-Effects

The final element of the Journey of Taste is the swallow at the end and the resulting aftertaste left in the mouth, coupled to any apparent after-effects.

This element is critical to the enjoyment of the product and provides enormous signals as to whether to re-visit the food or drink again – is it emotionally permissible to the consumer? It is the longest part in the duration of the journey and is less flexible. No matter how the product is eaten or drunk, quickly or slowly, the aftertaste remains the same. It is a direct result of the different tastes and textures in other areas of the journey and importantly how these tastes and textures have worked together – in harmony or not.

This harmony can be compared to the working of an orchestra. If any of the elements are too strident or dissonant in the orchestra, the effect can be discordant; the components – the woodwind, brass and so forth – must work in synergy to produce harmony. It is the same with the Journey of Taste as any discordant notes will be stronger and longer-lasting in the aftertaste. In addition, the other important aspect of the aftertaste is that it can build up. If it is persistent, repeated use will cause the tastes to be overlaid on top of each other and to increase progressively in the throat; too strident and persistent and the consumer will feel satiated. We saw earlier that the consumer will confuse strength of taste with quantity eaten; too strong an aftertaste and the consumer will not eat any more.

Therefore, the aftertaste needs to be just above the subliminal level – present but not dominant. For example, strong bitterness such as in dark chocolate or bitter alcohol is too much for most young consumers. Conversely, the younger consumers have learned to acquire the taste of artificial sweeteners, particularly in drinks, which their elders find chemical or metallic and very artificial. Any such notes will emerge in the aftertaste.

If a strong aftertaste is accompanied by a heavy feeling then many consumers feel guilt and excess such as after a heavy pudding or dessert. Unless consumed by males for immediate fuel, such foods are becoming increasingly isolated in the modern palate and only used for special occasions for the ultimate indulgence or treat.

The effect of feeling bloated – either from sickly, heavy foods or carbonation – can be very uncomfortable, more so for women when, for instance, consuming beer. The gas can be too much, causing repeated burping and a re-emergence of an unpleasant sour aftertaste.

So aftertaste and its associated after-effects can have strong, possibly negative, emotional associations for the consumers. However, there is another component which is equally more powerful and converse which we will deal with in the next chapter – the concept of Moreishness and its associates.

Chapter Twelve

Moreishness, Drinkability, Refreshment and Satiation

Summary

- Moreishness is defined as the response of wanting more of a product

- Taste intensity has a major role in avoiding the opposite of Moreishness - Satiation

- Chips are a classic example of a moreish product having a short duration of taste and drying the mouth

- The equivalent of Moreishness in drinks is Drinkability and Sessionability

- These both require that the drink has some stimulation but that it returns the mouth to its original state

- Both Moreishness and Drinkability are heavily influenced by even small changes in the Journey of Taste

- Refreshment on the other hand is all about liveliness and stimulating the taste buds

- Satiation is derived from high taste stimulation which lingers in the aftertaste

Moreishness is defined as a response to the food or drink that, once swallowed, encourages the consumer or even drives them to want to consume more of the same product. It is not when the consumption of one product creates the demand for another item to cause an in-mouth balance – for example salty snacks with beer. It is motivated to have more of the same and is very individually food-specific as it manifests in different ways in different foods.

It is derived from the nature of the swallowing of a food, a reflex action that is largely involuntary. At the point where the food item has been sufficiently chewed and received the full benefit of the in-mouth enzymes, it requires a specific act of will not to swallow. As a result, the consumer now misses the product's enjoyment and needs it to be continued. The key is that the food's taste delivery needs to be lost following the swallow or it will not be missed by the consumer. A strong lingering aftertaste is unlikely to be moreish. This is linked to the arrival in the stomach and the reaction to food that, for example, may be substantial in protein, fat or carbohydrate content or spiciness. Subconsciously this is linked to the taste hit and aftertaste to decide how much has been consumed. If the message is 'not much' then permission is given to keep eating – hence blandness, to a certain extent, works.

Taste intensity is very important because as the intensity builds up in the mouth, so do the feelings of having eaten enough start to emerge and the consumer feels full. As this begins to happen so Moreishness goes into reverse and the feeling of satiation begins prompting the consumer to consider stopping eating the particular product. They are too full or uncomfortable but this is very subjective and based on learnt experience and by the individual's value structure which causes them to say 'I do not like to feel like this.' Therefore, very strong tastes can fool the stomach into thinking they have eaten more than they believe; spicy ethnic foods or Marmite/Vegemite are classic examples. Conversely, sweet candy is generally the opposite as sweetness on its own tends not to provide satiation. Therefore, it is possible to continue to consume even though there is a lot of sugar sweetness in the stomach. Small children can continue to eat candy sweets until they are sick!

To understand Moreishness we need to examine the taste and texture of different foods and their effects. Looking at snacks such as crisps/chips as an example, these are consumed in a wide variety of Need States including making a break in activity. Here the major criteria are a front of mouth impact, both in texture and ideally a savory taste hit. This awakens and maximizes the change of mood by causing current thoughts to be discarded. However, if the impact is extended and prolonged to a degree it can promise a measure of fuel, sustenance and even physical energy. As the product moves from crunch to munch with the side molars, the texture changes until it becomes a chewed mass out of which strong mid mouth flavors can emerge. However, such savory snacks do not melt so they require transition to rear mouth chew and the intense tastes usually build up in the rear after hitting the front of the tongue through a powerful combination of salty, spicy sweetness. This has very little impact on the sides of the tongue which is why limited acidity can work so effectively from flavors such as vinegar or lemon/lime if the sourness is not too strong.

Most savory snacks are crucially very short in their duration of taste, exploding in the front to build up in the rear but without becoming so intense as to become satiating. If the taste builds too much, consumption will stop as previously stated and snacks need to be eaten non-stop until the packet is finished. You have to eat an enormous amount of such snacks to become full in the stomach. Rather, the taste receptors receiving strong, salty, sweet, spicy signals are more likely to become overloaded.

In such foods Moreishness usually comes from the drying of the mouth in the aftertaste, but the strongest character has been the habitual repeat of the front of mouth crunching. These two separate elements work synergistically to be very moreish – hence the worldwide success of snacks such as crisps/chips.

Sweet confectionery and foods work in a completely different way to snacks. Sugar carries taste very well through the mouth and when fruits are combined with sugar the result is magnified. However, fruit often produces acidity which can build up rapidly in the pit of the tongue, becoming satiating sooner than from the fruit flavor or sweetness. Therefore, sweet items need a low acidity to be moreish; however balance is required as if acidity is reduced, so is the taste effect and appreciation so a balance needs to be struck. Fruit flavors enliven and provide a gentle stimulation which is not particularly moreish; however if longer, smoother melt additions are used such as fats, then this can become potentially addictive.

Sweet foods with a powerful rich melt can be extremely delicious with the richness coming either from a release of melting flavors delivered in sequence and extending the melt or a light richness of sweet ingredient.

Cakes are an excellent example of the former while adults find the butter sweetness and rich creaminess of milk chocolate, which has a lingering and sticky melt but also bitterness to cleanse the palate, very moreish. Young children find pure chocolate too intense and satiating to consume in quantity, while dark chocolate has a similar effect for most adults. Indeed many use dark chocolate to ration their consumption of chocolate as the bitterness versus sweetness contrast is high, making the dark chocolate satiate.

Sauces are very interesting as they can enable a food to change its consumption occasion category. Meats can be made sweeter and more indulgent, difficult tastes can be smoothed out and long, rich delicious tastes can be created. In a casual eating culture this can promote the meal further up the hierarchy and significantly improve its appeal and frequency of use.

Such sauces stay out of the biting and crunching process but flow through the mouth with a good front of mouth taste impact for lively sauces and heavier, richer, possibly creamier rear mouth richness for calming, peaceful and relaxing products. Rich foods tend to be sweet but using herbs, spices and amino acids it is possible to deliver a sweet, rich effect without using sugar. As the sauce thickens in the mouth and slows its journey, so the intensity of mid mouth melt is increased. The longer this process can be made to last, the greater the perceived indulgence. Therefore, stickiness and resistance to dissolving will enhance richness and deliciousness.

However, the problem then arises that as richness increases so does taste intensity which leads directly to satiation from its overpowering impact. The consumer now starts asking 'Is this too heavy?' 'Am I eating too much?' – leading to a rise in discomfort and potential guilt. Therefore, it is difficult to create deliciousness and subsequent Moreishness through richness alone. What is required is a melody of flavors delivered in sequence, both light and heavy working in harmony. Balance is crucial as the flavors that deliver Moreishness if pushed too far can be satiating. The need is to produce products that deliver complexity without too much impact, richness without too much weight and deliciousness without too much sweetness or fat.

Examples of large successful worldwide products that have such appeal and are effective at delivering these are tomato ketchup and mayonnaise. Both these products have characteristics that in one instance avoid too much taste satiation and on the other too much sweetness and richness. So they are ideal with many foods; for example, in different parts of the world both are consumed with French fries plus an extensive range of foods.

Moreishness then in food products is a key component in making sure that more of a brand is consumed in one consumption and also that the food does not satiate and cause guilt which will prevent repeated consumption.

This brings us to Moreishness in drinks. Soft drinks, if they are fruit and acid based, are very refreshing but short in character in the mouth and are not moreish. They may have a richly rewarding taste experience but the consumer can easily tire of them. Orange, in its different drink formats, is gentle and has a mild acidic taste which does not dry the mouth excessively. Although more of the drink can be enjoyed without immediate satiation, eventually the taste and the texture builds and the mouth can become coated and too sticky. Drinks with lemon or grapefruit characteristics and flavor are never moreish as the acidity is too severe and astringent.

To introduce a moreish drink, richer taste elements that are almost heavy and substantial in flowing through the mouth are required which produces the characteristic of the melt, which in itself is moreish, plus if it can be rich and then clear the mouth easily, it produces an excellent continuous drink. It can be sweet, dry the mouth and must be syrupy-rich to create Moreishness. In carbonated soft drinks, the colas are excellent examples of a drink with such characteristics which contribute heavily to their global appeal.

Drinkability and Sessionability

Drinkability has completely different characteristics from Moreishness although the two have a relationship. Drinkability can be defined as the product being very sessionable so that repeated consumption does not tire the drinker – which is similar-sounding to Moreishness but is different. The key is that the drink must have balance in its character. So, for example, if it has a substantial taste hit in the front of mouth then it is required to have some bitterness and/or sourness in the rear mouth to counteract the front of mouth, so as not to radically alter the mouth taste state. If the drink takes the consumer on a complex journey in the mouth, it must be returned to more or less its original state, usually through bitterness/sourness which is interpreted as dryness in the mouth.

Sessionability requires that the taste journey has variation but is not excessive. Too much taste, even if it is complex, will reduce the sessionability. The sheer weight of taste, even if made up entirely of much-loved ingredients, will tend eventually to become too much. So at the heart of sessionability is the need for minimum aftertaste, or at least the aftertaste should be very fresh, clean, light and preferably elusive. What it must not do is progressively build up. It needs to diminish, and rapidly.

It is no surprise that the hotter countries have made the greatest contribution to sessionability in beers. There, self-evidently, quantity needs to be consumed for rehydration and so sessionability is a prerequisite. The biggest enemy of sessionability is excessive sweetness, excessive acidity or sourness. But bitterness at a low level can be effective in maintaining the thirst. Again, careful balance is required.

This dryness within the mouth therefore triggers the feelings of thirst and encourages the next consumption so the drink becomes highly sessionable – the secret of great beer brands around the globe!

Alternatively, the same result can be achieved with blandness. The drink needs to have a sensible pH with a low flavor level with all the elements of the drink not being broken down in the mouth and therefore traveling through the mouth with an easy flow. Milk is an excellent example with the fatty deposit left in the mouth continuing to make the drinker thirsty. It does not leave a clean, fresh or dry mouth but leaves deposits coating the mouth, which is not refreshing.

Water is highly refreshing but it has a similar effect to milk in that it simply washes through the mouth and neutralizes it, but does not leave any bitter, drying or even acidic taste. It is very difficult to drink a lot unless you are severely dehydrated. Those who try to adhere to the recommended two liters a day of water find it unnatural and difficult, requiring a specific regime and habitual self-discipline. However, imagine if trace elements such as minerals and salts were added, perhaps with a low level of easy fruit flavor. Although making it truly sessionable may be difficult, it would certainly add to its appeal and drinkability.

Temperature also has an impact on drinkability. Ice-cold drinks tend to neutralize the mouth and any significant taste impacts are reduced as is the sessionability. Hot drinks can be different. Tea cleans the mouth very effectively and the tannin plus slight dried grassy notes in the aftertaste produce a drying effect to make it easier to drink. Coffee, on the other hand, has a bitterness which is interpreted as dryness in the mouth which leads to a continuing thirst.

One important point to note is that for a drink to be sessionable it also has to be suitable to return to on a frequent basis. So a session is not just one occasion. A drink that is sessionable can be consumed in the morning and re-visited in the afternoon and evening with subsequent consumption. The mind recalls the initial pleasure and wants to repeat the experience.

Conversely, drinks which have a high acid initial impact, high flavor and high refreshment satiate very easily and when the consumer returns to the drink on another occasion, satiation will be likely to occur even earlier in the process. The result is that the consumer tires of the drink whilst they might like it initially and drink a great deal. However, after a while the pattern of usage and enjoyment will lengthen out until the drink is finally dropped and rejected.

Drinkability and Moreishness have a common difficulty for the brand owner. Quite small differences in the taste and mouthfeel, particularly those which influence the aftertaste, exaggerate the consumer's perception of the difference if they occur in critical areas. This makes it very challenging to get 'right' particularly as the target market taste palate and Need State fulfillment is constantly moving and evolving.

However, the potential commercial rewards of having a successful drinkable or moreish product make the challenge worthwhile.

Refreshment

Refreshment is interesting. This appears to be much more about a speed of reaction by the taste buds, with an item being detected with a great hit; presence and vitality will enliven the taste buds and produce a stimulation that is remarkably vibrant.

This could just as easily be a high-taste food that you crunch or it might be a drink. There are specific ingredients that have these effects. Saltiness combined with sugar provides this level of stimulation so does acidity which also delivers the archetypal refreshment which is astringency. Astringency is that rearward sides of tongue reaction when the mouth seems so dry that salivation follows immediately. The total feeling is one of stimulation followed by the watery effect of saliva.

Acidity tends to hit the pit of the tongue and this, if powerful enough, can add a very strong refreshing effect. This, for instance, is why sorbets are so excellent at cleansing the palate. High in acid, clear, uncomplicated in note and with sweetness to carry them through the mouth and provide an astringent rear mouth reaction, they are almost ideal. Interestingly, the consumer's judge citrus fruits by their acid level as much as they do by their flavor. However, excessive acidity satiates, and quickly.

Refreshment is also a function of liveliness. This is why lightly-carbonated drinks are extremely refreshing, the carbonation dancing on the tongue, creating a very similar response but twinkling across more taste buds than the astringency can do.

As the carbonation level is pushed up, so the taste is softened, smoothed, made easier. Drinks consumed through their heads, as are many beers, become kinder, easier, slower and less refreshing. If the drink ingredients are mid to rear mouth dominant, for example Baileys, then the refreshment will be at a very low level and the emotional response will be redirected, and far deeper. These characteristics stir the soul, relaxing and calming as previously discussed.

Satiation

Satiation itself is a surprisingly frequent occurrence, more so today as the consumer looks for more balance in their dietary intake. This is quite a serious enemy for a product; it is the opposite of stimulation deprivation. Here the taste stimulation is very strong initially and tends to remain in the aftertaste, then the next mouthful builds it even further. This provides an almost geometric curve of taste, building very rapidly until it becomes excessive.

It is a bit like too much newness. After a point the differentiation is no longer possible and this one mix of tastes is so prominent that the message goes into overload. Once that happens, of course, the individual simply stops eating or, indeed, they may switch to a drink to clear the palate, unaware that anything that had high refreshment or astringency would ironically be effective. If the flavor is really extreme they may even never try the product again. Ever!

However, if the taste that might normally provide the satiation is complex rather than inherently made up of one particular dominant flavor note, then this will reduce the satiation effect. Instead the individual will begin to pick up as certain taste buds become neutralized by the first flavor and a different emotional message will emerge. This often produces feelings of sophistication, reflection and quality. Complexity softens excess.

Satiation also has the effect of confusing the individual as to the level of consumption. The taste buds are telling them they have eaten or drunk an enormous quantity and this will overpower the 'not yet full' judgment of the state of their stomach. We judge how much we need to eat largely by the sheer volume and quantity of taste that we have appreciated. This means that high-taste items seem to fill more quickly and lower-taste neutral items, especially ones of interesting texture, do not have that effect. Popcorn is an excellent example of quantity being elusive to evaluate because of low taste and high texture.

Starch is used throughout the world to bulk up meals and also to provide a good balance between the stronger, more satiating flavors from cooked meats and the necessity to take on board sufficient really satisfying filling food. Tastes that are buffered assist in the consumption of food quantity.

As we discovered more about the different elements within consumption, it became clearer why all great dishes involve a combination of different strengths and styles of flavor, from the powerful to the bland, and how texturally they are also full of contrast. Additionally, it helps if by judicious use of eating implements you can alter the balance of taste between elements. This is something which one sees culturally, where the different ingredients are often actually served in different containers. This ability to mix also helps deal with the build-up satiation and allows contrast through different balancing of ingredients to occur.

Chapter Thirteen

Texture - Crunching and Chewing

Summary

- **Texture is a major determiner of how and when different tastes are released and experienced in the Journey of Taste**

- **Weight of the initial and subsequent chew signal different emotional messages**

- **The rear molars are employed when a harder crunch is required – which is highly stimulating**

- **Chewing conversely lowers the heart rate to be relaxing**

- **Generally, crispness is mildly stimulating, crunch is exciting, while heavy chewing suggests 'real' food values**

- **Consumers will often manipulate the food in the mouth to extract the maximum satisfaction**

- **The more flexible a product's shape and texture, the greater the likelihood that it will be used on more than one consumption occasion or situation**

Texture, or mouthfeel, of a food or drink is a major determinant of how different tastes are released in the Journey of Taste.

The initial bite immediately determines what teeth are going to be used to release the potential flavor. The weight of the bite and subsequent chew provide powerful emotional messages. The bite can encourage the consumer to keep going and repeat the consumption. So in a bag of chips/crisps the first crunch with the front teeth is very satisfying, stimulating and thought-provoking. It provides an alert mind and can change the mood and thought processes and can raise the heart rate and increase alertness. Intrusive, high-impact flavor is not essential, rather it is the repetitive crunching that is habit-forming and potentially addictive. The front and side molars are usually employed with some limited use of the rear molars.

However, with a harder crunch the rear molars are used to apply more pressure to release the flavor and break the texture. The crunch is highly stimulating but if too hard and too much effort is required then the consumer will worry about breaking teeth and the 'addictive' cycle is broken. Balance of texture is required to provide repetitive consumption. Give the consumer an initial bite that is substantial but not worryingly too hard, but with some cracking and crunching through the surface and you provide the impression of real food sustenance.

Chewing, on the other hand, will lower the heart rate, blood pressure and relax the consumer. This often assists concentration as it cuts out other distractions in the mind. It also provides salivation so it continues to be effective even if the taste has disappeared, and the resultant calming and relaxing emotions can be quite compulsive. Chewing gum is an obvious example.

Crunch and long chew products should be viewed as a continuum, with blurred divides between the sectors. This is because these meanings are 'learned' during the growing-up process and as this varies by society so the emotional response will also vary. So what is crisp in one country may be a light crunch in another. For example, the US has a very soft food palate with smoother flavors. Therefore US cheese products are extremely mild, soft and creamy by world standards.

In general terms, crispness is mildly stimulating, promises lightness of eat and healthiness. Crunch is exciting, intrusive and dynamic, awakens and promises a powerful taste hit and some real food values, while a heavy chew or munch suggests 'proper' food, no snack values and serious substance.

Light crunch is personified by chips and cereals that either dissolve rapidly in the mouth or form a soft bolus of food swallowed swiftly. The chew is brief.

Hard crunch, short chew items like Nachos and some salad elements, many fruits and vegetables fit in here as do peanuts or cashew nuts and cereal bars. The chew needs the molars and as an aggregate is formed, some oils or fat elements should help the chew-out as lubricants. Emotions will vary here greatly. Most confectionery is here, so is popcorn, as are fast foods US style, which often mix crisp and soft textures successfully so substance is transitional but often fun.

Hard crunch, long chew is serious. Roasted nuts are here, so are hard cheeses on biscuits as is steak and French fries. When these foods have a real taste hit the consumer feels very satisfied and can satiate well before they are actually full. Saltiness adds to this effect, as does the burnt outside of roasted surfaces.

The food should be contextualized in terms of when first experienced in life which will determine its perception for life and the values surrounding its usual consumption – if it is serious or fun, a naughty snack or proper food.

As mentioned previously, the texture and how it dissolves will largely determine how and when different flavors are released in the mouth. However, the consumer will often manipulate the product to extract the maximum personal satisfaction to fulfill their emotional requirements. Products can be nibbled, crunched, licked, sucked, used as a mouth toy, and moved around different parts of the mouth to optimize satisfaction in the desired consumption occasion. The more flexibility a product's shape and/or texture offer, the more likely it is to be used on more than one particular occasion.

In confectionery terms a solid, heavy chewing bar is more likely to be used as fuel by men or possible indulgent eat by women. However, products which can be consumed in a number of ways, through texture and shape, offer more flexibility. Kit Kat and M&Ms are classics used as 'on the go' snacks, ritual eats, with a drink, me-time and indulgence amongst others by different age groups and sexes.

Chapter Fourteen

The Melt

Summary

- **A powerful source of emotion occurs when the food reacts to chewing and temperature, moving taste and texture from one state to another**

- **As the Melt occurs different flavors are picked up by different receptors in the mouth**

- **This is often a powerful emotional trigger signaling indulgence and relaxation**

- **Rich sweet foods are an example but so are some savory foods such as cheese**

- **Both the rate and weight of flow through the mouth are important determiners of deeper relaxation, slowing the heart rate**

- **The balance of the nature of the taste, sweetness, fat content and syrupy dissolve will determine the level of emotional impact in the Melt**

We now come to one of the most powerful sources of emotion in the Journey of Taste – the Melt.

This melt occurs when the food reacts to the stimulus of the chewing process, the temperature of the mouth on the melting of the flavor through the enzymes in the flavor. The melt is a critical transition where the taste and texture move from one state to another into a liquor whose speed of melt and richness flow through the mouth and signal the emotions which are going to be generated in the Consumption Experience. If these emotions are positive and fit into the consumer's perceived value structure then the experience is appreciated.

This is a powerful determinate of preference for as the melt occurs alternative tastes are picked by different receptors in the mouth. The sequence and the change from one taste to another have a strong influence. Individual taste notes are unlikely to be identified, apart from those which are very obvious. Rather, it is the journey of these tastes which is emotionally significant.

Frequently this is a powerful trigger and in-mouth experience, linked heavily to the individual's relaxation and indulgence. It can change a mood so much that people's eyes move out of focus as their thoughts become inner-directed in the moment. When supported by the appropriate tastes and mouthfeels this can be a difficult behavior to stop. The user, once the emotional escape from the experience has stopped, will be dragged from their reverie and emotional escape once the mouth is empty.

The desire to return, or more likely to maintain by repetition, encourages the consumption of more of what has been eaten. Obviously many of the rich sweet foods deliver their emotional peace through richness and sugariness. Cakes and chocolate are prime examples. However, savory foods are equally capable of delivering such emotions through the melt and with less associated guilt. Cheeses are an excellent example as are rich, creamy sauces which can work well with neutral carriers, such as pasta, to deliver complex and rich melts.

A lot of foods melt at mouth temperature and flow through the mid mouth, coating the tongue and roof of the mouth. The rate of flow through the mouth is very important as well as the feeling of weight in the mouth. The slower the flow, the deeper the relaxation, the more profound the state of reverie and the greater the escape from existing thought processes and concerns. That is why heavy alcoholic drinks and desserts, providing after dinner depth and sweetness, are part of the mood change. Cognac, Baileys, gateaux, Death by Chocolate and Irish coffee are prime examples of how these emotions are delivered.

This melt can slow the heart rate, reduce blood pressure and help relaxation enabling the enjoyment of the tastes to be heightened in the Consumption Experience.

It can be seen that the balance, nature of taste, sweetness, fat content, richness and syrupy dissolve of the melt will have various levels of emotional impact. As discussed, not only does the texture, richness and weight of the dissolve signal messages and set up emotional release, so do the flavors themselves which have different emotional connections learned through life. How many of the emotions are found within the texture of the melt, or in the flavor and do they work synergistically or sequentially?

As the impact of flavor and mouthfeel varies with different foods, in different parts of the mouth, so do the emotions. The emotional journey is the reward and that is why the taste is enjoyed. This can be a difficult and complex journey to decode and deconstruct but can be done.

Example of How Different Products' Emotional and Physiological Delivery Work

Chocolate

The key to chocolate is its melt.

As previously referred to, the reason we coined this word melt was that the first time we discovered it was with chocolate. As a reminder, a firm, fat-based solid melts within the mouth, both by temperature and enzyme action, and goes from solid to rich syrup form in only a few moments. As this happens, the taste seems to get deeper, more complex and profound. Then, as it sequentially hits the taste buds through the rear of the mouth so the complexity, creaminess and richness cause consideration, reflection and, in excellent examples, reverie.

These are particularly rewarding, indulgent and comforting experiences and because as they are slow, they are much more noticeable and have a longer-term effect. The consumer remembers them, delights in their return and is captivated by the flavor and emotional outtake. Unsurprisingly they return, seek the experience again and a loyalty towards the taste structure begins. The emotional delivery is very powerful and consumption can become compulsive and much more can be consumed than planned, particularly by women. The comfort obtained can be especially powerful when the women consumers are upset and seeking solace which can lead to even more consumption. It is noticeable that the speed and rate of consumption when women are angry or upset is faster but then slows with increased consumption to a 'regular' rate as the chocolate melt delivers comfort and slows the heart rate (it is interesting to note that men often do the same thing with alcohol!).

Generally, the whole objective for women eating chocolate on a regular basis is ideally to make the experience last as long as possible. However, they are less likely to do this in public for fear of embarrassment or mess, whereas in the privacy of their own home they seek to extend the pleasure and therefore chocolate is eaten in a number of ways to maximize this enjoyment in the home.

For example, often a piece is bitten in half and allowed to melt in the mouth. The melted chocolate is then pushed against the roof of the mouth to melt further and coat the roof with chocolate. The tongue is then used to lick the residue of chocolate from the roof and other parts of the mouth.

Alternatively the chocolate is placed in the mouth and slowly sucked and rolled around the mouth while larger strips are often licked like a lollipop. The chocolate is often either refrigerated or melted on a radiator depending on how the chocolate is preferred. Colder chocolate will take longer to melt and is therefore more likely to be licked or eaten in small pieces while warmer chocolate extends the effect of the melt and increases the impact.

Soft centers such as caramel are bitten or nibbled around the edges and then the soft center is either licked or sucked out with the remaining chocolate placed in the mouth to dissolve slowly.

Therefore, to maximize the consumption experience chocolate pieces should be designed to fit into these eating methods. In particular the piece should be as easy and as non-intrusively smooth as possible plus allow the individual consumer the ability to eat in different ways to maximize enjoyment.

The ideal pieces or chunks of a chocolate bar are easy to handle in both the hand and, more importantly, in the mouth. A smooth shape with no sharp edges works well with the soft texture and easy melt allowing the consumer the ability and flexibility to suit their mood. When timed, a piece can take between 15 and 55 seconds to consume with the average being about the mid 30 seconds.

Chocolate pieces which are harder with sharper edges require harder work and more effort from the consumer. Most try and smooth out in the mouth by chomping or continue rolling around the mouth until the sharp edges have dissolved and softened.

Men mostly eat chocolate in a completely different manner. The key requirement is to maximize the satisfaction by chomping and chewing to gain food values. Chocolate bars are often used as 'fuel' and a sugar energy boost by men particularly 'on the go'. Therefore size more than shape is a key requirement which is why countline bars are popular amongst men – they can determine the size and quantity of an individual bite. Chunks give them less flexibility but still provide chomping and chewing satisfaction while more curved chunk shapes can potentially be seen as feminine and therefore open to rejection. In addition, a number of forces which have already been touched on in previous chapters have combined to influence chocolate's appeal to consumers:

- You are what you eat
- Greater body image awareness
- Changing consumer taste palate

This has led to an overall eating strategy which controls the intake of 'treats' – indulgent or semi-indulgent foods which are usually (but not always) sweet, leading to the consumer evaluating the emotional reward versus the desire for the treat based on this strategy. Such beliefs can alter the taste plate, where 'too sweet' or 'too much' provokes suspicion and guilt, redefining judgment and choice. In chocolate the consumer will often seek to try and enjoy the treat but limit the consumption. One method is to switch to dark chocolate consumption from milk chocolate. The bitterness in dark chocolate builds in the rear mouth to a level which is unacceptable to many which self-limits consumption.

Bagged bite-size packs and products also fit logically into this paradigm. However, this can potentially be part of a major self-deception by the consumer, which leads to a suspension of beliefs if the 'correct' signals and rules are present.

To begin with the bag must not be clear – the contents, particularly quantity and portion size, must be concealed otherwise this potentially signals worry over control and potential guilt before the product is consumed. The quantity and size of a bar of chocolate or candy is obvious whereas a bag is difficult to judge which helps the consumer in their self-deception.

The breaking open of a seal increases and intensifies the expectation and pleasure making it difficult to reseal, but the option must be available, as again the ability to control will be questioned. The major consumer self-justification for bite-size bags is that some can be eaten now and some can be shared later so a reseal is important. Indeed, amongst families there is some sharing; however, the bulk of the product is usually consumed by the purchaser who is often the heavy user of the product. (It is similar to married couples who 'share' a bottle of wine where the husband often drinks two-thirds or more of the bottle!).

Flavor builds up in the rear mouth and aftertaste leads to signals of satiation, where the body is 'fooled' by taste intensity to believe that it has eaten more than it has. This in turn leads to feelings of guilt. So the mouth must be cleansed after each portion of bite-size otherwise repeated consumption will be challenged.

Such Moreishness (the desire to consume more of a product) can be accomplished by the inclusion of cereals, nuts and sugar candy coating – even with products that have chocolate as a major component. Such products can send a message of being 'light on the hips' enabling increased emotional reward as they cleanse the mouth.

What is clear is that chocolate retains its powerful emotional meaning and delivery to the consumer and they will seek ways to enjoy the experience within the boundaries set by their emotional and physiological value structure which will in turn, as previously discussed, impact their taste palate.

PART THREE

Chapter Fifteen

Need State Categorization

Summary

- People need to classify and organize information at both the conscious and unconscious levels

- New experiences are related and categorized versus other similar experiences

- This enables Need State categorization, the Need State being defined as the motivation for the Consumption occasion

- For food and drink this is a set of practical, physical and emotional requirements for a specific eating and drinking occasion

- The problem (and opportunity) for brand owners is that Need States are open to almost continuous change

- A traditionally popular product can be rejected as its emotional fulfillment is not appropriate for the evolving consumer's lifestyle and value structure

It is part of the human character that people need to package, classify and organize the information they receive – at both a conscious and unconscious level. When faced with a new experience, consumers automatically try to relate and categorize versus other similar experiences which they understand. The new experience is classified as either similar to something they are familiar with or different from previous experiences.

This storing of data into categorized pigeonholes helps the individual control the learning process. Once classified, the retrieval of this data is as simple and as swift as possible. This classification is given an encrypted description of three or four words which can encompass good, bad, indifferent, modern, traditional, safe, dangerous or whatever the individual has felt emotionally. Once the experience has been classified it does not require much re-examination as whenever re-encountered it comes with a list of short word descriptors and attached emotions, it is familiar and known, allowing the individual to operate in a relative comfort zone to be used or rejected.

In marketing, this process is called Need State Categorization, where Need State is defined as the motivation for the consumption occasion. In food and drink terms, a Need State is a set of practical, physical and emotional requirements for a specific eating or drinking occasion. This classification or categorization is very extensive. Is the food eaten to refuel you, neutralize, refresh, provide mental stimulation, relieve boredom, relax or excite? Is it fun, mainstream, everyday, for special occasions and for whom?

The consumer will go through this process, much of it at an unconscious level, by recognizing patterns in the product presentation. This could be two or three signals that stir the unconscious memory – perhaps packaging, name or key descriptors. If the product involves the individual's self-image, will it reinforce that self-image or not; 'What will others around me think, does it send out the wrong signals about me?' All these and many more types of questions will occur at an unconscious level; there may be a couple of inputs which require conscious thought for a second or two, but they are then pushed to the back of the mind.

The problem for the brand owner is that these Need States are mostly open to an almost constant process of change. Not only do the individual's internal requirements of the Need State change or evolve, but so do society's. The importance and frequency of occurring will alter; it will mutate and evolve or may even disappear. It is likely that a food or drink is not being consumed in the same Need States as in a previous generation. Life has changed enormously from formal meal locations and a semi-limited diet to a massive choice, individual meals, grazing and an awareness of the balance of diet. 'Is this food good or bad for me?' The result is that eating Need States have been revolutionized over a relatively short time, which is very apparent in different generations. How many of the young adult generation drink gin and tonic? Or Scotch and ginger ale?

Younger people prefer lighter, more frequent, high-taste experiences whereas older generations prefer longer, slower, richer indulgence. It is very difficult for the brand owner to appeal successfully across the entire age range of men and women. Food and drink, therefore, have a substantial fashionable aspect to their acceptance. This is driven more by the change of Need State than it is by a brand aging or reaching maturity in its life cycle. The Need State underpinning a brand becomes less appropriate to the society of the time. Its taste and textures become inappropriate due to the emotional meanings they signal and no amount of repositioning or repackaging will change that; it needs reformulation or a completely new product to deliver the consumer satisfaction required for today.

If we take heavy, rich, indulgent foods as an example, such as pies, puddings, cream cakes, gateaux and so forth, even the sight of such a product can trigger the rich, heavy feeling as it melts in the mouth and the anticipated weight in the stomach of replete satisfaction. To a consumer looking for relaxation, deep comfort and escape this is immensely attractive and very indulgent.

However, if the consumer wants a sweet, clean, light taste to end a meal then the above desserts are just 'too much' as they provide too much heavy bulk and are too substantial for requirements. They are also seen as fattening from the visual cues of richness and sometimes implied calories, as a source of potential guilt.

Therefore, this emotional rejection towards fulfilling an indulgent Need State fits many individuals' idea of the modern, healthy lifestyle. However, yoghurt can be appropriate and permissible. Alternatively a small amount of cheesecake or cake can fulfill the same sweetness, fat and calorie content as the yoghurt, but this is often rejected. Why? Because what is being rejected is the guilt, being associated with the actual in-mouth taste and texture of the cheesecake or cake, not the true nature and number of calories.

Even though the cake is attractive to many, its emotional fulfillment is not appropriate for the Need States of today's consumer lifestyle; therefore, it can force rejection unless the guilt is suspended for a 'special' occasion which gives permission to consume.

Chapter 16

Understanding Need States

Summary

- It is important to understand how, what, where and why a product is consumed in a particular occasion or situation – its Need State

- Generally most brand owners draw their boundaries at five or six Need States to avoid complexity

- Many successful brands emigrate from their initial Need State to other uses and occasions

- However, it is imperative to understand exactly why the product works in its primary Need State(s) plus what it is replacing and its competitors

- Therefore a complete understanding of the physical and emotional benefits versus competition is required

- To ensure the needs of different age generations and light users, many brand owners work on portfolio management

- This is achieved by building and adapting their core products' taste and texture to be more relevant to their wider target audience

The concept behind Need States (defined as the motivation for the consumption occasion) is to find out how, what and why the consumer eats or drinks a product in a particular occasion or situation. This depends on how many Need States are defined and how narrow or wide their individual scope. However, in general terms most brand owners draw their boundaries at five or six Need States for their product or product category.

More than this and mapping can become too complex and microscopic.

Most brands begin their consumer existence by being eaten in a narrow and specific situation, as fuel or sweet indulgence. However, if consumers find that a product provides satisfaction in one area, they will tend to start using it in other areas where the product was not initially intended or positioned. Many highly successful brands emigrate from their initial Need State to generate usage in other and varied occasions. After all, Coca-Cola was initially launched as a product with medicinal properties! Many products evolve their delivery, flavor options, quantities, presentation formats, packaging, sizes and so forth to migrate the product into additional Need States – for example, from a bar for fuel and energy to a bite-size pack for 'on the move' snacking.

However, in order to accomplish this it is imperative that the brand owner understands exactly why the product works in its primary Need State. How is it eaten? Is it nibbled, crunched, sucked or chewed? Is it eaten alone or with other items? When – at what time? Fundamentally what are the emotional and physiological requirements being met by the product in that Need State?

In addition, what does the product replace, what is its main competition and what makes the competitors work and deliver satisfaction?

To achieve all of the above there needs to be a complete understanding of the taste delivery, the physiological, psychological, practical and emotional benefits of the product versus its competitive set in the identified Need State. Against this background it must be acknowledged that society and culture are constantly changing and that will often have an impact on identified Need States. The size of the Need State can grow or diminish, old ones die and new ones are created. This can be a source of opportunity or a potential problem to the brand owner depending on their ability to adapt, re-align to, respond to or even formulate a new Need State for their marketplace – for example in the area of Better For You/ Good For You pharma-foods, potentially turning an everyday product into a problem-solving solution or preventative.

Changing age cohorts will obviously have an impact on Need States. As the eating and drinking habits of a society develop and change, so different age cohorts will have different values. (Note: They are changing at an increasing rate.) A core of loyal users may age and not be replaced by new ones, causing the product to diminish or even die as new users may have a different set of values.

It seems inevitable with different generations that their requirements and lifestyle are radically different. Certainly the tastes they have learned to associate with different emotions will be different from those of previous generations. Therefore, when consuming they will have and use different criteria to evaluate the experience, based on different learnt responses to flavor.

This new attitude to an existing brand can cause potential problems in that the new generation's reaction to the physical and emotional stimulus generated by consuming is likely to differ. If a product's appeal is limited and possibly unsatisfactory then the brand will have problems meeting consumers' needs in its future unless the product is modified to meet the new criteria of evaluation.

This poses a problem to the brand owner: do they modify and hope it does not alienate existing, particularly heavy users, or take the risk of an uncertain future with potentially loyal users 'dying off' and the brand foundering? It is a function of many marketers' careers that short-term results are preferred to potential long-term gains.

However, based on our wide-ranging experience, the loyal user is very tolerant of changes made within the eating and drinking experience provided some important principles are adhered to.

Key to this is retaining the core tastes and mouthfeel within the product supported by appearance and particularly its aftertaste. If these elements are seen in the context of the c120-160 tastes and mouthfeels we identify as part of our work that are common in most products, the core values can be identified and retained while building new tastes which appeal to the younger consumer who has different emotional and physical criteria for judging the consumption experience. The product can, therefore, be made more contemporary without alienating the core loyal user.

The same principles apply to light users. These can be very difficult and frustrating for conventional market research to reveal and understand fully. These are consumers who dip in and out of the product, consume infrequently and do not engage or identify with the potential emotional delivery. A possible answer may lie within the nature of their Need States. Many do not have the motivation or desire to be in the identified consumption occasion that makes the product of value. Only on rare occasions is the product valid for their need and therefore consumed. However, they often eat similar or competing products in a similar occasion, therefore there must be a problem which needs to be resolved.

If in our approach for this example we ignore brand values or image, this can limit use because the consumer does not identify with the emotional values of the brand. If this is discounted, then within the 120-160 tastes and mouthfeels we identify there may well be tastes and textures which stimulate negative emotions or physiological reactions which put the consumer off. The flavor is associated with a bad memory or experience, the mouthfeel makes them feel fat and guilty, the aftertaste is artificial and unnatural, the color is wrong for the product and puts them off, the shape is too small and childlike. There could be a myriad of reasons but essentially these are within the product, flavor, aromas and mouthfeels which have negative connotations they do not like, not because they are inherently unpleasant but the messages they generate are negative. The key is identifying and understanding, and placing them in the context of the emotional delivery in the desired Need State(s).

There are some tastes which a nation or culture has not acquired and they will almost immediately reject. Liquorices notes, cinnamon and, surprisingly often, coconut for example, are found to be difficult, strong, pungent and penetrating amongst many western markets. A hint of these 'weird' tastes present will cause rejection as if striking a wrong note in music, potentially turning a prospective heavy user into a light user or even rejecter.

To answer the needs of different age generations and turning light users into heavy users, many organizations we have worked with focus on their brand portfolio management, building and offering a range of products based on their core product in a more targeted and appropriate manner to the consumer. So brand owners could, and probably should, have brands within their portfolio that appeal to younger consumers to lay a trail of taste signals which will lead them to their core product as the consumer matures.

So for example, as we have seen, children's tastes favor simple uncomplicated tastes with easy messages which are relatively unsophisticated. Therefore a brand owner can offer a simplified version of their product to appeal to children but contain some of the key core messages within taste and mouthfeel, albeit toned down.

In a perfect world, ideally the brand should also have a teenage transition product. These years are very powerful in forming new attitudes. As the need for a teenager is to be perceived, by themselves and their peers, as adventurous so teenage products need to be different in some manner from the norm. So a number of chip/crisp brand owners offer exciting, different and frankly weird flavors in their range to appeal to the teenage market. However, underpinning that taste is the core textural message of their brand which also has appeal for the adult market.

The result is that the 'old' established large brands have a younger version of the product, possibly slightly repositioned but aligned for each generation to enable them to enjoy its discovery. However, each product feeds into the core product to build the brand. It is practically impossible to build a product that can stay in the same form from cradle to grave. Alternatively, you can build a Taste Signature® which can stretch into that period. Many teenagers drop their teenage transition products when they move into adulthood as these are not products which can take them further into a brand portfolio. If the taste signals and Signature were carried forward into an 'adult' version then this would become less of a challenge.

These same principles can also be applied to healthier diet or increasingly more functional food versions of a brand with a specific health positioning. The danger is that when trying to stretch a brand into these new Need States, to justify the claims much of the flavor and texture delivery message is lost as the fat, sugar, salt or other ingredients are removed.

If the messages and signals relating to the core brand are at too low a level then it can lead to severe dissonance and questioning of the core brand values. On the other hand, many brands need updating; indeed most successful brands owe their success to the appropriateness to fulfill a Need State at the time of launch. However, as discussed previously, new generations acquire a new taste palate which has different emotional meaning and values.

Each generation, therefore, is evaluating a product differently in terms of their response and reaction and this can easily be in a negative direction. Yesterday's wholesomeness and nutrition is today's too stodgy and fattening; yesterday's taste complexity is today's unnatural and artificial; yesterday's comfort is today's over-indulgence. The list can go on and on but it inevitably reflects upon the majority of food and drink brands in some way or another.

These changes in perception and the devaluing of individual taste and mouthfeel characteristics are a major component in most brands' life cycles. However, subtle tuning of the product can have a remarkable effect with the brand rejuvenated without seemingly major changes. Firstly, the Need State needs to be thoroughly investigated and understood in delivery for the target market to provide a direction as to the likely problem and difficult areas. Then the individual tastes and mouthfeels responsible for the changing values and perceptions need to be thoroughly detected and understood. Once these are understood then by careful analysis and development of the process, formula or recipe, it is possible to reduce the negative taste signals and boost or add to the positive taste signals and therefore the emotional messages desired by the consumer target market to achieve preference.

Remarkably, usually very little has to change to make a brand or part of a portfolio relevant to the target market. In hindsight this can be seen as unsurprising as the previous success of the core taste messages and Signature is probably built around long-term emotional values. All that is required is to build and adapt the tastes and textures to make the brand more relevant to the changing consumer of the identified target market.

Using the correct consumer market research methodology these messages can be analyzed precisely and then re-engineered through taste and mouthfeel to match the consumer requirements to ensure the continued commercial success of the brand.

Example of how a Product's Emotions and Physiology Deliver

Stimulating Snack Need State

Stimulating Snack is an example of a Need State, in this case being met by a chip/crisp.

In order to stimulate, a food needs to have a very clear and obvious first taste. This needs to be strong, easy and not too complicated. To carry that taste, either sweetness or saltiness or a combination needs to be present. The salt will stimulate the taste buds and accentuate the taste and the sweetness will help carry that flavor. Fat can be used, but in low quantities; if it is excessive, the texture will be inappropriate.

The texture needs to be nibbly, crunchy and involving the front teeth. Preferably this process should be noisy and intrusive so that all the senses, including hearing, are involved. This initial crunching and fast taste delivery awakens the mind.

By triggering the mind in this way, it stops it thinking about what it was preoccupied with immediately before the crunch. It provides an opportunity for a change of thought direction. Because of the pace with which this crunchy, high-taste, small-piece snack delivers, it will speed up the thinking process and therefore make the person feel more alert. They then become more awake. This awakening starts the break.

The items within the product need to be small, possibly eaten one at a time or a few crammed into the mouth together. Their taste needs to be identical. If there is a variation in taste, then that will stop this generation of speed of thought and cause the person to stop, reflect and diagnose what all the different tastes are, which is too intrusive. Equally if the product was too difficult to select from its container and deliver into the mouth, that would again intrude and the stimulation would be lost. This must be a very fast eat.

The product then needs to dissolve in the mouth pretty quickly; if it ends up being chewed as a heavy mass by the molars, then it is becoming too food-like, too substantial.

In that instance, the message the mind picks up is that here we have a real food item which is going to provide fuel and satisfaction and represents a real meal. At that point, if that were so, the consumer would start to re-classify the product and it would no longer give the signal 'snack' and the fun would start to evaporate. Now it would be fuel or sustenance, and serious.

Because the snack provides this change of mood it is positive and upbeat in its character; it then is ascribed as fun, entertaining and enjoyable. It changes pace, provides a break from the mundane and gets rid of the responsibilities.

It is essentially an irresponsible break in time and as such very enjoyable and welcome. It is fun. It fires the child within us to delight and we recall it fondly. When we eat it again the fun is re-triggered.

Also of course you will probably finish it before you are ready to. So the pack is gone almost before you are aware that you started to eat it. This again provides a break and accentuates the level of stimulation. Should you eat it for too long, then the taste would start becoming predictable. The stimulation would slow down. The taste buds would become tired. The effect would evaporate.

It is no surprise therefore that these products are usually contained in small bags, they are never individually wrapped and they are more savory than they are sweet. They are high in taste. Because stimulation and newness is more attractive to younger people they tend to be eaten more by younger people than older ones. New, dangerous, intrusive – just ideal for a teenager. Guess who usually eats them?

If you put too much complexity of taste into the product it becomes more sophisticated and requires more thought. If you package it too carefully you move it into more formal occasions. If you make it too perfect you can deliver the crunchiness but now you are delivering a measure of evaluation and indulgence. Yet again, you move the product away from that original particular Need State. It now invades a new Need State.

Let us not imagine that all snacks are stimulating and we can see at once that the stimulating snack has to have certain ingredients. If they are not there or the product is too sophisticated or complex, it will move out of that Need State and become something else. Perhaps a Sophisticated Social Snack for parties or similar more formal occasions?

Chapter Seventeen

Mapping the Taste Signature®

Summary

- To measure and utilize emotional messages requires a unique methodology and process

- The Encounter must be first understood plus the product's subsequent usage journey to the present day

- How this has developed and changed over time needs to be mapped and analyzed

- In addition, what is the product's competition and what has it replaced?

- After that the exact tastes and textures and how they are delivered need to be understood

- The emotions then produced in the experience from these tastes and textures are then analyzed

- These emotions are then matched to the individual characteristics of the Taste Journey's experience

To consciously recall a taste, people conjure a mental picture in the mind. It is very difficult to recall the taste of, say, Spaghetti Bolognese without a mental image. Tied to this image is an emotional connection, either conscious or unconscious, and these emotions view the eat as either negative or positive. This, as we have seen, can be linked to the circumstances of the eat or its first encounter and their effect on the learnt and associated emotions. The balance of the messages will determine the emotional response to the consumption. It is that emotional response that will determine preference.

So as a brand owner how can you measure and utilize these emotional responses to improve your competitive position in the marketplace?

As a commercial company that has researched emotional taste preference over the last 25+ years we have developed unique tools and methodologies which must remain commercially confidential. To fully understand how and why a product is preferred (or not) it is essential to understand the experience of the first Encounter and its subsequent development. At what age, who introduced it, with what other foods and beverages, in what location, circumstances and occasion, how first consumed etc. They all work together to create a complete individual picture of the Encounter.

The next step is to understand how the consumer behavior towards the product and competitors evolved over time during the life stages of the consumer until the present day. Did they stop and start, why, what did they use instead, why did they restart? What were the occasion and circumstances and so forth, in what manner was it consumed? Have they continued to use it in the same way to the present?

An examination of present day behavior leads us directly into Need States.

As previously mentioned, understanding Need States is critical. The concept is to find the different circumstances in which the consumer eats or drinks the product. Clearly it depends upon definitions as to how many Need States you will find. Generally speaking, most companies tend to work with five or six Need States per category.

If a greater number is selected, firstly it can restrict the ability to grasp the totality of the market due to the resulting complexity. Secondly, it is very difficult to market operationally if the Need States become too small in their share of consumption.

We learn from studying the Encounter that most brands begin their life with the consumer by being eaten in a very specific situation. This might mean as a component within a specific meal, it may be as a stand-alone item eaten for pleasure, indulgence, comfort or to provide energy and fuel. It might even be a displacement activity with high tastes and crunch simply to give people something to do. This is a great way to beat boredom.

From building a picture from the Encounter to present use the need is to understand exactly why the product works in its primary Need State. How is it eaten? Is it nibbled, crunched, chewed? Is it eaten alone or with other items? Is it eaten in sequence with other foods? How are other flavors and the Journey of Taste through the mouth working in that Need State? What are the psychological and emotional needs of the state and how does this product, in detail, deliver those as an eat?

It is also important to know what the product has replaced, what are its main competitors, and what within their eating experience makes them competitors and successes in that Need State. Often an evaluation of the key ingredients and their Need States provides great insights.

To do this there clearly needs to be a complete understanding of the taste delivery, the physiological, psychological, practical and emotional benefits of the product versus a competitor's and, of course, the total Need State.

It is useful to find out when the product was launched and what consumers expected from its advertising, packaging and conceptual idea. This can be compared to what was delivered in reality once they started to consume. It is also imperative to understand whether this Need State is growing within society or is on the wane. If it is growing, from where, i.e. from what other Need States is it stealing?

As consumers enjoy a product in one Need State, they will tend to utilize it in another Need State for which it probably was not created. In reality, nearly all highly successful brands migrate from their initial Need State to populate a number of others to generate significant scale in the process.

Because specific tastes or, indeed, quantities of product or mixes of flavors tend to restrict a product to a Need State, it is often wise to look at other tastes, packaging sizes and presentation formats in order to evaluate the product opportunities in other Need States.

A final thought on Need States is that as constantly as life develops and changes, society moves on. The Need State sizes wax, wane and new ones are created. This is an area of major competitive opportunity. These changes can create important opportunities to launch new brands and reformulate and reposition existing brands to optimize consumer preference over the competition.

We then move on to understanding the exact tastes and textures in a product and how they are delivered to the consumer.

As we look deeper into the psychology created by the taste, we begin to learn many ways in which we can utilize this information. It gives us an insight into the brand's relationship with the consumer, not otherwise grasped at all. It is a different dimension. It communicates to the unconscious. It motivates and persuades. It is at the very heart of the loyalty of usage.

Whilst you might wear the brand – indeed many do – as a way of expressing to others your value structure, you are wholly conscious of this but the enjoyment of the product itself transcends such values and works at a far deeper level.

The shape of the taste encapsulates the impact upon the consumer of the different elements within that taste. They may be textural, such as mouthfeel, or they may be flavorful. The important thing is that as the product is eaten, or drunk, and moves through the mouth, so different tastes and different flavors impact at different times in their journey and the emotions move with those changes to provide, for those products one likes, a familiar and entirely positive experience.

We have seen how those learnt values remain with the consumer for extensive periods of time, decades even, and it is those that guarantee the continued consumption and enjoyment. They only fade when a more appropriate or relevant series of emotions is driven by a new taste experience used in the same Need State.

The more contrast there is between textures and flavors, the more the emotions are moved and developed during the eating, and the more likely the product is to be popular and successful. Bland food and drink items tend to be more staples, providing bulk, background or length to other tastes. They may soften them, buffer them and make them last longer or ease them, but they are not the star. The hero of the eating experience is this powerfully emotive taste journey. So the taste journey and shape must be right and completely understood.

As the impact of flavors and mouthfeel varies with different foods in different parts of the mouth, so do the emotional responses. These can attract, involve and captivate us. The emotional journey is the true reward and why we like the taste of a food or beverage. However, the apparent source of the taste message can be concealed, moved or marked. For example, lemon is detected in the pit of the tongue while lime, its close relative, to the rear of the mouth. Dairy fats move the apparent impact of a flavor towards the rear of the mouth while sweetness accelerates the flavor's early recognition. This is why sweetness will usually always improve the initial response to a food (remember the sweeter Pepsi taste challenge versus Coca-Cola).

It provides an early, clear taste message as well as being popular in itself. Acidity carries notes to the sides of the tongue but carbonation will widen the area and increase the intensity of impact.
Therefore, although flavors have specific taste buds to detect them, the degree of sweetness, sourness, acidity, bitterness or dairy fat can cause the effect of moving the impact of taste to different parts of the mouth.

Temperature also has a great deal to do with taste impact. Extremes of cold or heat significantly reduce many flavors. The richer tastes normally perceived more at the rear of the mouth will be reduced while front of mouth tastes will stand out. However, sour and bitter notes survive temperature extremes quite well while sweetness is tempered.

This reduction of flavor delivery does not mean that sweet, salty, bitter, rear-acidic notes will lack impact. Their flavor is reduced when chilled but taste elements still remain which enhances refreshment. For example, with lemonade the higher acidic content creates more of an impact, saliva is increased and the result is refreshment. In reality the cold drink has stimulated the refreshing flavor response but not actually delivered true refreshment.

Another example is taste intensity which, if delivered powerfully, can fill up and satisfy consumers largely irrespective of the 'weight' of food in the stomach. Evidence suggests that consumers stop eating when they have received sufficient taste. This is done without judging the sustenance or calories, as with Indian and Chinese foods for example.

QEP Shape of Taste®

The QEP Shape of Taste® is a diagrammatic way of illustrating the impact upon the consumer of the different elements of flavor and texture. As the product is eaten or drunk and it moves through the mouth so different flavors and mouthfeels impact at different times in that journey. Emotions move with these changes to provide a familiar and positive experience for the product that the consumer likes. We have seen in earlier chapters that the learnt values can remain with the consumer for a long period and it is those that generate continued consumption and enjoyment. They fade easily when a more appropriate or relevant set of emotions driven by a new taste experience is used.

Therefore, the QEP Shape of Taste® is key to a product's usage, Need State satisfaction and inherent popularity. This experience and the emotions produced from the appearance, aroma, flavor, mouthfeel and aftertaste through to the after-effects on the stomach have to have contrast and variety. The more contrast there is between texture/mouthfeel and flavor, the more the emotions are moved and developed during eating and the more likely the product is to be popular and successful.

Bland food and drink tend to be more staple items in a diet. They provide bulk plus background to other more exciting tastes which they may soften, ease or make last longer but such bland items are not the star – for example pasta without sauce or added flavor. Humans always need contrast in their enjoyment of experiences. Therefore, foods or drinks need to have these contrasts present so that at some moments it might be sweet, at others sour, hard or soft, crunchy or easy, rich or light tastes and textures.

A product's QEP Shape of Taste® therefore needs to contain enough stimulation for people's emotions to be involved and stirred to make the product appealing. Consumers want these emotional changes to maintain interest and avoid boredom. Diet foods often fall into this trap, lacking flavor and contrast which many find worthy but dull and therefore soon tire of.

If the food has a very strong front of mouth impact, either through its texture or taste, then it will awaken the consumer. This makes it appropriate for Need States where people want a break in their current thinking to relieve them from boredom, or a way of holding their concentration during a repetitive task. When the taste has a slower, smoother flow and it moves through the mouth with richness and weight, then the resultant reduction in heart rate produces a relaxed, comforted feeling.

Many of the great commercial tastes have both characteristics within one experience, making it possible to utilize the product in a number of different ways. Therefore it can be used on a host of different occasions where the emotional requirements are different and so the product is effective across a multitude of different Need States.

QEP Shape of Taste® - Granola A

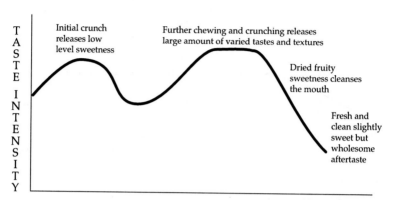

T
A
S
T
E

I
N
T
E
N
S
I
T
Y

Initial crunch releases low level sweetness

Further chewing and crunching releases large amount of varied tastes and textures

Dried fruity sweetness cleanses the mouth

Fresh and clean slightly sweet but wholesome aftertaste

DURATION OF TASTE

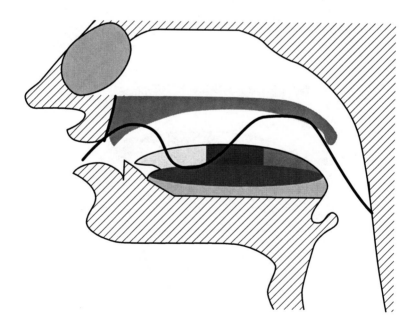

QEP Shape of Taste® - Granola B

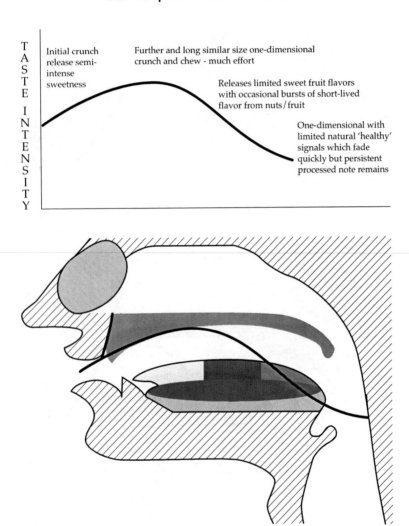

TASTE INTENSITY

Initial crunch release semi-intense sweetness

Further and long similar size one-dimensional crunch and chew - much effort

Releases limited sweet fruit flavors with occasional bursts of short-lived flavor from nuts / fruit

One-dimensional with limited natural 'healthy' signals which fade quickly but persistent processed note remains

Overall, the first product example shows a complexity of delivery in both taste and texture as a second release of flavor is generated in the mid to rear mouth, while the second is a one-dimensional delivery where further effort from chewing is not rewarded with further taste and complexity. Both products start from an initial crunch but soon change due to the balance and complexity of ingredients, the first product reaching increasing and higher levels of satisfaction while the second product fades into a slow decline. Unsurprisingly, the first product is a major consumer favorite and commercial success while the second has been withdrawn from the market.

Chapter Eighteen

Utilizing the Taste Signature®

Summary

- **The Taste Signature® is a methodology and system which helps brand owners understand the taste delivery of their brand**

- **Within the multitude of flavors and textures there is a key core that is most evocative**

- **Combining these critical tastes and textures with the key emotions produces the Taste Signature® of the brand**

- **This can help a raft of marketing initiatives such as advertising, packaging, existing product reformulation, brand extension and portfolio management as well as NPD**

- **In short, all areas of brand development**

Understanding the Taste Signature® is therefore vital to brand owners. This knowledge is of more value than any other aspect of understanding the taste delivery of the brand. It can even help with cost reductions or new processes, and can make sure you remain true and faithful to the brand that the consumer knows and loves. It is so easy, without this understanding, to move outside it and make multiple errors. Unfortunately, this is quite common. Brands that extend beyond their core competence can become damaged as their core message is weakened.

The Taste Signature® is a methodology and system which helps brand owners to avoid these mistakes and, at the same time, take full advantage of the brand and product strengths. A Taste Signature® is a corporate asset.

Here is a Taste Signature® for an actual chocolate item as an example

Milk Chocolate Bar - Taste Signature®

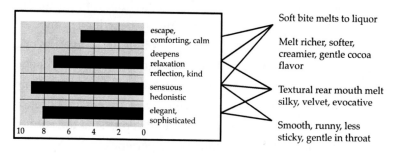

Emotional Benefits Prioritized   **Taste Characteristics**

On the left are the emotions the consumption has created and their relative levels of importance. On the right are the key elements of taste, flavor and mouthfeel with the connecting lines showing how tastes trigger and drive these emotions. The bars on the left are not empirical but indicate the relative level of importance of the key elements in the Taste Signature®.

The Taste Signature® can also be used for product bite size and shape, and particularly as a guide for line extensions. It may help other elements of the marketing mix and Need State targeting. Advertising agencies often find the analysis particularly helpful in building greater product insights into creative briefs to assist in a brand's positioning.

Within the multitude of flavors and textures there will be a core key few that are the most evocative of the delights of the particular food or drink, such as: the smooth complexity of malt whisky; the melt of a pure chocolate bar; the rich slow warmth of Irish Cream; the wonderful crunch and powerfully persistent taste hit of Nachos; the explosive shattering at the heart of the most successful snacks; the crisp into soft bite at the beginning of a chocolate countline bar.

All of these are at the core of the Taste Signature® of a particular product, but they are never as simple as described above. It is always a combination of a critical few four or five flavors, some textures – maybe a couple – and the movement or change in taste through the shape that together makes up the Taste Signature®. You could easily describe it as a fingerprint because it is a unique profile of the product that represents the core of the personality of that consumption experience.

However, of equal importance is that by fully understanding the consumption it also reveals the summary of the emotional deliveries that the product evokes.

It should be noted that the core of the eating or drinking experience is a limited range of key tastes, mouthfeels, aromas and aftertastes that make up the heart of the consumption appeal. They are likely to be effective in all the Need States, but it will be the peripheral flavors that help the product realign itself for consumption in different states and occasions.

In summary therefore, combining the critical few tastes and textures and the key emotional values they evoke creates The Taste Signature® of the brand.

Consumption Contract

An example of how this can be demonstrated is the Consumption Contract – a chart which shows the relationship with the core brand positioning and how different range extensions can fit into that relationship or not as the following example shows.

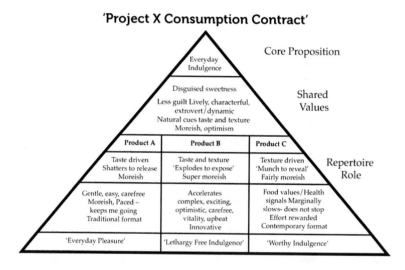

'Project X Consumption Contract'

Once you know and fully understand your Taste Signature®, it can drive a raft of other marketing initiatives, for example in advertising strategy because the information is available for the real reason for consumption and can be utilized; however, it is best done in an oblique fashion. Since these emotions are held at an unconscious level, if the message is played too strongly and obviously, the consumer will feel insulted and intruded upon and will reject the message; so it needs to be executed subtly and carefully.

Advertising is best used by exploiting the emotions of the experience, but leaving the taste message alone. We know that consumers are much more comfortable thinking in emotional terms, or at least they are in the western world. Therefore the message is best carried out at that level where it will be credible, acceptable, understandable and persuasive.

It can also be used in terms of packaging, either picking up on the emotions, which can come through the packaging, or utilizing appropriate colors or graphics to help communicate the taste without using the language. Taste is communicated very effectively by color and also by shape, and this is a very good way of completing and fulfilling the message.

The real core benefit of understanding the Taste Signature® is for the development of the brand. Once the Taste Signature® is completely internalized by brand owners, it makes it possible for them to extend their brand. As long as they remain faithful to the key Signature, they can change the other elements within the brand and still remain true to the main cause of consumer loyalty.

This means the consumer recognizes that taste immediately as belonging to that brand, even though it is in a new format or even a completely different Need State or other food category. This makes it possible to take a brand that is relatively small or, indeed, dominant in a small category and grow it elsewhere. Today, with the costs of launching/generating new brands being so high this is almost certainly the most effective way of moving a brand forward.

In this way you take the Signature, you know the priority of different elements of the Signature, and those that you might be able to bend a little, and so extend the brand's reach and product formula. For example, if you had a rich sugar- and fat-based melt as part of the brand, there would be nothing to stop you utilizing a biscuit melt or even a cheese melt to produce the same effect. In this way the brand could move into radically different areas but still carry the true message at the heart of the taste.

The consuming process is a potential area for major misunderstanding. For example, with products which were traditionally always eaten or drunk within a range of different occasions and locations but there may be potentially other areas often well distanced from the obvious. Usage often evolves as Need States develop until it is quite distanced from the original understanding. This can, and frequently does, lead to wrong pack sizes, wrong individual product sizes and incorrect levels of flavor, carbonation and even alcohol.

This faulty perception is usually built on by flavor line extensions. These deliver tastes, configurations or sizes that, through their journey within the mouth and, therefore, the emotional response, bear a decreasing relationship with the way in which the original flavor is consumed today. They can be too far from the Taste Signature® which can lead to a confused consumer who will look elsewhere for their satisfaction and fulfillment.

Chapter Nineteen

The Final Tuning

Summary

- Once the Taste Signature® is understood the taste of a product can be finely tuned or optimized

- This can be represented in detail by a Taste Brief – a key output used extensively by both Marketing and R&D

- Particularly in product updating and NPD where an existing product is not appealing to the changing taste palate

- It is surprising that even slight tuning can potentially have a dramatic effect

- It can have the effect of turning the Taste Journey from discord into harmony

The final tuning, once the major taste characteristics with their messages are fully understood, is the process of tuning the taste. A major client coined the phrase 'Optimization' for the process that we carry out. Quantification can be used to ascertain preference but tends not to diagnose the basis of that like or dislike. However, using our qualitative method that works with both taste and psychological profiles, we can soon find that the shortfalls tend to be provided by the delivery of negative messages which reduce the appeal.

Once these have been brought more in balance by careful debriefing of R&D technical people, then the message can be carefully re-engineered through the taste to match that which the consumer requires and indeed tunes in well with the positioning of the brand itself.

Once the food or drink is evaluated, it is then a case of describing in detail which parts of the taste, mouthfeel, aroma or aftertaste are successful, understanding why and delineating those that require change or resolution.

From this it usually follows that R&D are well able to make the changes necessary to bring the product absolutely in line and optimize the taste and emotional message. Experience shows that when test samples are produced they should deliberately bracket the requirements by both under- and over-shooting on some of the characteristics in order to judge degree and range of change.

Once the taste has been optimized then quantitative research provides confidence to go into various sizes of market test on the way to the product's revision, re-launch or even a new product's introduction to the marketplace.

A key output which has been of immense value to clients is the Taste Brief. This lays out clearly in consumer language guidance to allow the brand owner to optimize a product's development by allowing different departments such as Marketing and R&D to work from the same language and brief.

An example of the visual and narrative dimensions is given overleaf.

A Typical Taste Brief for a Drink Product

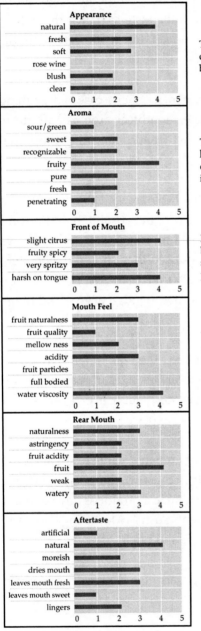

The drink is natural in color, it is cloudy. It is a pink/red blush and looks both soft and fresh

The aroma is fruity and fresh because it has sour and sweet notes in good contrast. This makes it smell fresh and it is recognized

It is very light but also extremely fruity but sweetness is at a low level - this suggests the drink is natural juice in pure spring water

The thin nature of the drink makes it mellow but the real fruitiness is reinforced by the acidity - the fullness of fruit mouthfeel is also there

An important area for emotional response, here the light but acidic hit produce an almost cider-like astringency - again suggesting the naturalness of the ingredients

This drink has a taste that lingers just as fruit does, leaving the mouth fresh with slight dryness in the rear of the mouth at the sides. All of this screams natural and the sweetness/ dryness creates a moreishness - such a drink would be both refreshing and rehydrating

A major area where such a taste brief can be exploited is in product updating.

Almost all successful brands owe their success to the appropriateness of the food or drink to the time of their launch and during their subsequent life. However, since each new generation learns a new taste palate with different emotional, psychological and physiological meanings attached to certain of those key tastes, so the physical and emotional benefits generated by a product can change over time.

Each new generation, therefore, is potentially tasting a different product in terms of their response to it and, as this meaning evolves, it can move too easily in the wrong direction.

Yesterday's wholesomeness is today's too fattening. Yesterday's complexity is today's unnatural. Yesterday's comfort is today's overindulgence. The list goes on but it affects every single product in the marketplace.

These changes in perception and devaluing of individual taste characteristics are an undoubted component in a brand's life cycle. However, subtle tuning of the product can have a remarkable effect. The brand can be completely rejuvenated without appearing to the consumer to have undergone major changes. The Taste Brief can demonstrate exactly how such changes can be incorporated into an existing product's formulation and at what level.

In Conclusion

As previously stated, Need States need to be completely understood to see what they are doing in terms of demand for delivery and movement within the user groups. This will give a clue as to the likely areas of problems and difficulties.

It is absolutely imperative that the individual tastes or mouthfeels responsible for those changes in values are detected. Also, at the same time it is essential to understand that the core Taste Signature® does not need alteration, it needs exploitation.

The taste journey should be seen as a melody. If the woodwinds in the orchestra play a little more softly then the strings emerge more overtly. This is the art and science of tuning taste to fit current emotional values.

From the above and in the preceding chapters we have attempted to show the power of the Emotions of Taste – how they are formed, work in practice and can be measured and utilized to achieve Consumer Preference for food and beverage brand owners to achieve competitive advantage.

For more information and continuous updates, please visit our book website www.thetastesignature.com which is intended as an information resource on the Emotions of Taste.

Appendix -

QEP Need State Orbits®

Orbit One - Snacking

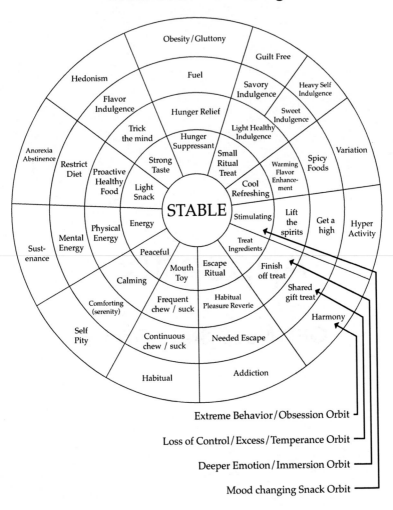

QEP Marketing Clinic has developed its own Need State categorization methodology and models to help with Need State categorization. These are based on Orbits of Emotional Fulfillment in an eating motivation/occasion and this example, Snacking, shows how such categorization works.

The inner circles are fairly functional and do not fulfill a huge Emotional Need. However, as we work out of the Orbits we see that the Emotional Fulfillment and Need become higher until we reach elements of extreme behavior and Emotional Need on the outer Orbit.

Orbit One

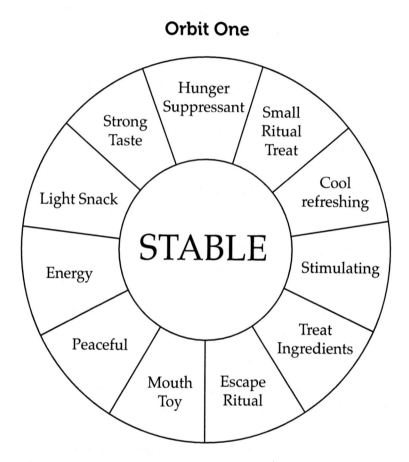

These are the classic Snack Need States and all can be imagined to have a perfectly understandable and reasonable benefit to a consumer.

Orbit One is the basic Usage such as having a snack or similar which takes the user into a fairly benign state of Mood Shift – a physiological and emotional re-set before the next activity with no loss of control.

This results in foods utilized within the Mood Changing Snack Orbit being regarded as healthy, frequently pleasurable but totally socially acceptable.

Orbit One Need States Snacking Examples

A piece of toast with Marmite – **Suppresses Hunger** and **Strong Taste**.

A two-bar Kit Kat – **Small Ritual Treat** – can nibble, bite or suck to gain – **Stimulation, Mouth Toy** or **Escape Ritual**.

Chips give both **Strong Taste** and **Stimulation** and also help **Suppress Hunger** – hence their success.

A little cream cheese on a crispbread is **Cool Refreshing** but also a **Small Ritual Treat** (the Melt). It is also a **Light Snack** and has **Stimulation**.

A single biscuit with tea/coffee can be **Stimulation** if bitten or **Peaceful** and **Escape Ritual** if it is dunked.

Even a small ice cream qualifies – **Cool and Refreshing** but it must be small – while a yogurt is excessive as it is too creamy. **Light Healthy Indulgence** – a probiotic yoghurt, however, is a healthy **Light Snack**.

Even a single square of chocolate is a snack **Small Ritual Treat,**

Strong Taste. To be perceived as a snack the product must be available in a single serve overtly snack-sized format.

Orbit Two
Deeper Emotional Immersion

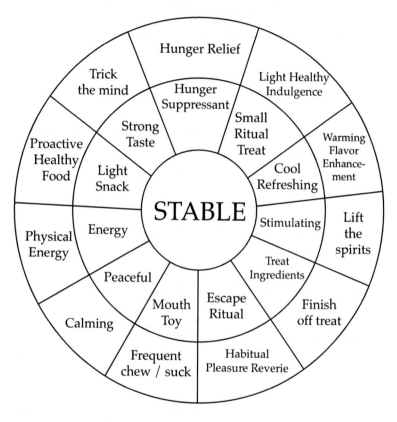

Beyond the immediate emotional rewards of a snack lies a deeper emotional requirement for psychological support – from similar items or small upgrades.

As the pressure on the consumer is to resolve that emotional need or as the emotional reward increases in attractiveness to them, so the snack evolves into something quite different.

Within this second Orbit of Need States we find the consumption of snacks goes beyond simple innocent moments into behavior that has a stronger emotional underpinning which we describe as immersion in Orbit Two.

This is when the behavior may become socially unacceptable – consumers may conceal the need and its resolution.

This is now a significant behavior addressing a deeper need – and the brand loyalty is geometrically greater.

Stimulating shifts to **Lift the Spirits, Hunger Suppressant** to **Hunger Relief** – a step beyond the physiological requirement to more than is strictly required, which invariably means more is consumed.

The product delivery is often better tuned to the emotional need via additions.

Some Orbit Two Need States

Hunger Suppressant via a few bites of an item now evolves into **Hunger Relief** with a serious need for a greater calorific intake and volume of food, and firmer chew.

Because of the pause between consumption and bodily awareness that food has been consumed, the quantity is likely to be in excess of what is actually required. This is why slow eating reduces hunger.

The snack has now evolved from a brief need to a more significant and substantial one – eat two snack-size units and the divide is crossed – 'I have eaten two biscuits' – but in fact five may have disappeared!

Previously, some interesting crunchy items, possibly with good high taste impact, would provide **Stimulation** but here in our second Orbit more is required to **Lift the Spirits** – the chip is high-flavored or now dipped, the chocolate a little more special.

This demand for a greater emotional delivery by the food inevitably means an increase in the quantity and often variety of the food needed to overcome the emotional negative of feeling a little down and possibly bored.

This applies to all of the Need States from Orbit One (which were Snacks) into Orbit Two where the need, and indeed intake, has geometrically increased and the product is often a more luxurious alternative to the snack – Control is being lost.

The **Small Ritual Treat** becomes a **Light Healthy Indulgence** and interestingly Ferrero Rocher is in **Food/Treat Mix** and not a **Sweet Indulgence** product, hence its success.

Orbit Three
Orbit Three Need States – Loss of Control, Excess and Intemperance

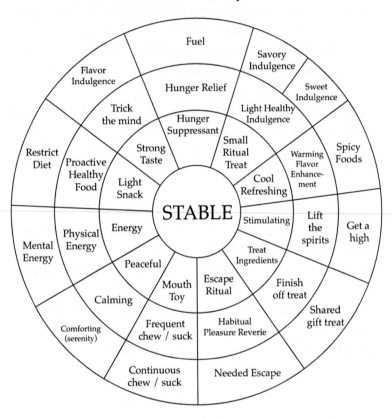

Here the need, while fundamentally still the same, has evolved until the pleasure from the food, its taste and texture and its in-mouth experience is delivering an experience well removed from the initial snack.

The consumer is experiencing an inability to restrict the consumption because their emotional needs for the reward often dominate their self-control.

The person becomes lost in the experience. This reverie is the peak moment and will be recalled; it can be melt, heat, warmth, long taste with a consistent flavor level.

This growth of the Need State, from an innocuous snack through to a serious need, means that the foods that are effective (and known to be so by most consumers) do not have the same image and social and personal acceptability.

Orbit Three is Excess where an overwhelming (at that moment) emotional need is satisfied.

Consumption at that moment is not restricted because the need for the reward overwhelms self-control and the consumer is 'lost' in the moment of the experience.

However, frequency of use in this mode may be restricted – it needs to retain its specialness.

Orbit Three Need States

If we use two dimensions as examples, **Hunger Suppressant** was extended to **Hunger Relief** and is now **Fuel**.

This means that the quantity must be substantial within the mouth, the product needs to be really bitten into, must be a heavy eat and arrive at the stomach with weight, substance and real presence. If

this is not so, then the requirements of Fuel Need State are not being met.

Also the metamorphosis of the **Savory** and **Sweet Indulgent** Need States is another good example.

Commences as a **Small Ritual Treat**, a couple of mouthfuls of something you fancy – evolves to **Light Healthy Indulgence** – a small delicious upgrade.

But now it has morphed into either **Savory** or **Sweet Indulgence** with an emotional reward which is **Heavy Self Indulgent**.

Outside Orbit Three – the Emotional Drivers of the Behavior

Each Orbit moves more slowly than its inner neighbor as it has less frequent consumption occasions along with progressive upgrades of brand/quality of ingredients at each Orbit.

Everyone has permission to use the outer Orbits – but if they are used to excess, social pressure increases and there is social censure.
Frequent use can also suggest unattractive characteristics found either within yourself or within the image others would have of you.

So 'a little of what you fancy does you good' but an excess of it can show (by today's values) loss of control and the emergence of unfashionable social behavior.

The Indulgence Need States

To explain in more detail how such Orbits work, we can take the example of indulgence states before moving on to look at those that do not commence within the inner Orbits as indulgent but become so by the time they are in the outer Orbits.

Small Ritual Treat

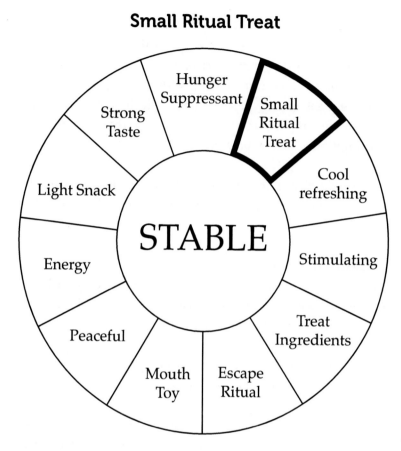

Mood Objective

This is eagerly anticipated and is frequently from within a narrow range of food items which tend to deliver a similar emotional reward.

The reward is for job done or time served through the day and represents a closure to a certain spectrum of tasks before this classic short break.

It is seen as earned reward and legitimate satisfaction.

Physiological Objective

This is all about oral and flavor satisfaction enhanced by the selection from a short repertoire of absolutely preferred items. Hence the consumer can enjoy those things they most treasure with the greatest pure pleasure and with the absence of guilt because the impact on the stomach and the awareness of consumption will be almost non-existent.

In this experience the lift from the sugar kick moves the consumer out of the previous mood into a fresh invigorated start.

Ritual/Timing

Ritual is critical here; if the person is on their own they are likely to sit in the same chair with the same issues around them, i.e. a drink with the food and the desire that everything is 'just so'.

If it is shared with others then it is still important that all of the above factors are correct and in place.

The product is unwrapped in a similar fashion, eaten in an unhurried way and the process maximized in duration in order to enhance the value of the experience.

Mood Journey

The mood journey begins with a rejection of the previous state of mind, followed by a period of calm relaxation and then followed by a feeling of a fresh beginning.

Classic psychological states are passive to active, quiet to optimistic, reserved to social.

Food Characteristics (tastes and textures – their effect on mood)

Items involving small sensible bite with good sweetness, complexity of **Small Ritual Treat** texture and often lightness of impact – alternative general direction is richer, heavier, more succulent, strong melts that relax and give a measure of escape but are controlled by the quantity consumed.

The product must have an image of everyday availability, quality and not be over-packaged or scarce.

Light Healthy Indulgence

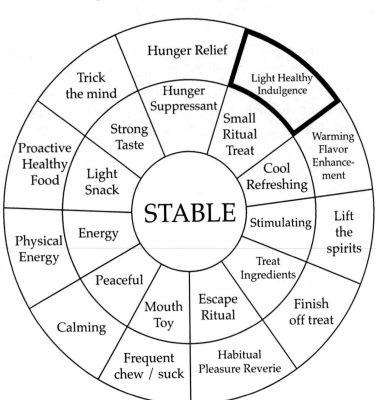

Mood Objective

A careful balance between the desire for the emotional delivery of full indulgence but leavened either by the use of acknowledged healthy ingredients or by restraint into the amount consumed.

Physiological Objective

The product needs one of the ingredients to be relatively full in mouth, creamy, succulent and spread throughout the whole mouth surface area. This maximizes the emotional reward, especially the deeper emotions, but by restricting consumption or using healthy ingredients the consumer takes the pleasure (but not to excess) and has the qualities that the stomach will be aware of arrival but still be hungry; the consumer will therefore feel righteous, justified and rewarded.

Cereal bars, yoghurt, nuts, dried fruit and low-fat items deliver the control that this Need State demands.

Ritual/Timing

This is a classic occurrence for women after children are dropped at school or mid-afternoon before collection, or in the evening – but the last is more difficult to control.

Again the ritual will be quite substantial – the right plates and cutlery, the right chair, the right moment, the right TV/radio program or music, perhaps even magazine or book.

The ritual then becomes rewarding of itself because the taste experience and emotional rewards become paired psychologically with the ritual behavior and therefore reinforce each other.

This makes it possible to carry out the ritual behavior but with a reduction in the amount of product or use of healthy ingredients and still achieve the same rewards. Control is therefore very substantial and this enhances the pleasure.

Mood Journey

This is a deeper mood journey.

Calm, peaceful, reliable, at ease with oneself – rewarding stolen moments and feelings of mild excitement, a little reverie but a largely guilt-free experience.

Food Characteristics (tastes and textures – their effect on mood)

These will always be rich, have sweet content (although it may be a single ingredient that is sweet), high-fat content in order to give the lusciousness and the flow through the mouth – chocolate is frequently involved but yoghurts, cheeses, fruits and crème fraiche are all also very effective as a partial ingredient.

Items such as mayonnaise have the right image to fit this occasion without producing guilt but do produce the in-mouth melt and flow through.

Interestingly, flavor is not as important as texture here and the melt is the key but without stickiness, substantial weight or excess sweetness.

There is no loss if the item is savory but has sufficient taste bite to satisfy and slightly stimulate which mirrors some of the satisfaction and stimulation from sweetness.

Savory Indulgence/Sweet Indulgence

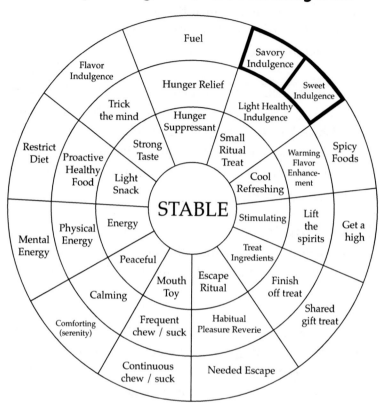

Mood Objective

Here the consumer desires an extended period of hedonistic pleasure maximizing the deeper emotional rewards of peace, escape and flights of fantasy.

Physiological Objective

For this Need State, which is at the top of Pure Indulgent development, the mouth must be filled with rich, heavy, preferably sticky, frequently sweet, soft material.

Contradiction between ingredients is not really acceptable. Complementary taste/texture is the most effective format, also where it is the same pure ingredient repetitively or they melt together and the result is delicious.

This product will impact heavily in the stomach leaving substantial aftertaste. It is almost imperative that the product is moreish and its real weight will be felt in the stomach to the point of repleteness. Indeed, for many individuals there is only emotional satisfaction and true emotional security once the stomach is significantly filled.

Ritual/Timing

This is ritualistic but not in quite the same fashion as the lighter forms of this Need State – it occurs less often to retain its specialness.

One ritual is in the steady spooning of the product into the mouth, often before the previous mouthful has been swallowed – a slow quiet eat. Another is when the product is not rushed through the mouth, is dissolved or sucked.

Where products have to be unwrapped then often this occurs while the previous identical item is being consumed.

The ritual shifts from the chair, the environment and time to the ritual within the consumption itself – which is now the hero; if this is being shared (dessert), the oral satisfaction takes people to their own world and reverie.

The consumer has abdicated to the eat itself and control has been surrendered, often in a social sharing setting amongst friends.

This occurs most frequently in the evening and is often carried out while watching TV and can indeed be enjoyed alone late at night as a moment when the senses are more aware of sensuality and hence the pleasure is maximized.

It is no coincidence that this sensuality has sexual overtones and hence chocolate is a starring item amongst such consumption – but chocolate is not the everyday choice.

However, sweetness is not anything like as important as creamy, full mouth feeling and, indeed, excess taste tends to intrude into the slow, steady development of this escapist self-indulgent mood.

Mood Journey

This is a journey of which the consumer is totally conscious and revels in the total introverted hedonistic process.

It takes them from boredom, loneliness, lack of excitement or adventure on an absolutely guaranteed journey of textural fulfillment, inner peace, calmness and significant peaceful satisfaction.

Unsurprisingly, like many of the outer Orbit consumptions, this is

addictive and a moment of personal worth – 'I believe I am worth it until consumption ceases!'

Food Characteristics – Sweet Indulgence

Eaten with the fingers or from the spoon is the optimum.
The product must be soft, possibly aerated, smooth, rich, sticky and stay in the mouth as long as possible.

Secondary characteristics that melt but demand minimum chewing are totally acceptable, as are hot/cold mixes, chocolate/fudge/ice cream.

As a carrier for other ingredients pastry is ideal since it melts with the food – so many desserts are a perfect example.

Excess sweetness, sourness or bitterness is counterproductive as these three characteristics build up in the taste and begin to dominate, create satiation and the individual has to stop before they are replete, so the satisfaction is incomplete.

Products, therefore, should not possess excessive intrusive tastes or indeed very strong coloration outside their natural color spectrum.

The Consumption occasion can lead to feelings of lethargy, being bloated and unhealthy – even overweight.

This makes guilt very powerful indeed and so anything that assuages that guilt, i.e. reduction in sweetness or strong taste, is an important supporter.

Also the self-indulgent nature of this experience can make people ashamed and, as a result, secretive and therefore conceal the habit which again can be powerfully compulsive.

Food Characteristics – Savory Indulgence

Savory foods, however, carry far less guilt and do not require concealment as they are socially acceptable.

Examples would be a rich stew, a deep and soft Yorkshire pudding, foods with wine, creamed potatoes.

Between the needs (these Orbits), the key ingredients are soft breads with butter and cheeses.

Soft cheeses more than hard, creamy more than crumbly – a variety is ideal; high-taste notes do not work here with wine or fortified wine adding significantly to the descent into reverie, satisfaction and calm relaxation.

These taste/texture and especially mouthfeel characteristics are the same as for Sweet Indulgence.

Savory, however, gives 'Permission to Indulge'.

Flavor Indulgence

While this springs from the Strong Taste snack it is a different idea and the indulgence is not of the full in-mouth but satisfied by a strong flavor.

Mood Objective

The mood objective here is ever-greater hedonism and enjoyment of the superb flavor.

Physiological Objective

This is an in-mouth oral satisfaction combined with olfactory flavor impact to provide an overweening, intense and extensive experience. In order to achieve this taste level, a reasonable amount of consumption is needed but also demands either fat, sugar or alcohol to carry the flavor.

Ritual/Timing

This is ritualistic in that it will be habitual in the way in which it is treated, the same consumption process being repeated in the same manner. This is frequently a shared consumption and not so much one of solitude because talking about the taste and the occasions on which it has occurred mean that it adds to the enjoyment.

Often these products are only available in their optimum from retail outlets and therefore ethnic foods have a powerful presence here and the ethnic environment or venue, whether it is restaurant or take-home, becomes part of and core to the ritual.

These ethnic foods demand different side ingredients to complete the experience.

Mood Journey

This is an exciting upbeat experience.

There are strong party characteristics and this is a talkative, interactive community event – McDonalds is an ideal example.

The community may only be the family or friends but it is the collective experience with the learnt behavior that goes with that experience which is part of the ritualistic enjoyment.

This is interestingly addictive but, strangely enough, can be overdone as individuals need rest periods between these events so that the newness of the experience is honorably reflected; this was a discovery and it has to remain a form of event.

Food Characteristics

Often food which is at its best when freshly produced. This is because the high, volatile taste and flavor notes get lost and staleness destroys the experience.

Foods, therefore, need to be original, different and unusual and have some association with location or lifestyle in order for them to become a part of that event.

Interestingly, all these foods involve high sugar content, often extremely well concealed, to help carry the taste. Also the fats used are saturated for the same taste reasons; this leaves deposits in the mouth which do not clear and are part of the reason why people require a rest between consumptions.

Calming

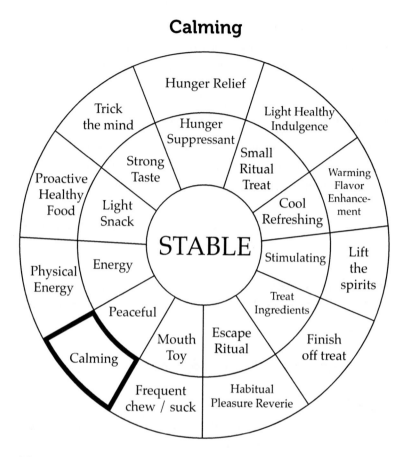

Mood Objective

To bring peace, a measure of serenity and calmness to the individual in an acceptable and controlled framework.

Physiological Objective

The ingredients and the eat work together to slow the heart rate and relax the individual.

This can be done through steady chewing or even biting, combined with an eat that creates an aggregate that becomes sufficiently smooth to provide a satisfying swallow.

It is the combination of the chew, the aggregate and the swallow that produces the calming, heart rate reducing effect – it can be done with chewing alone and chewing gum is a classic example of this Need State.

Ritual/Timing
There is little ritual here; the main process is that the chew provides the ritual for the body and the mind, the timing is very flexible and can be used as and when required.

As people's need for calm tends to be diurnal, there is a time of day issue when there is a greater requirement.

Mood Journey
The mood is from feeling stressed, under pressure, even mild panic through to calm, peaceful relaxation.

This is an effective method of mood control.

Food Characteristics
The main requirement is that the food eats well into a good bolus and then flows through into a fine swallow.

This, for instance, is the reason for the Ferrero Rocher success which also helped separate it from excessive indulgence and therefore gives permission to eat.

The consumer does not see this mood as addictive or loss of control or anything about which they need feel shame.

Comforting

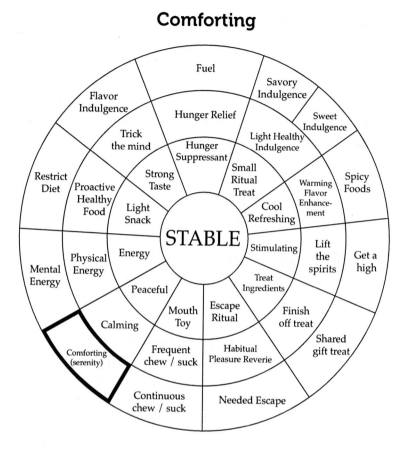

Mood Objective

In this dimension consumers are trying to find serenity out of anxiety or out of fear.

People who feel undervalued in any way, temporarily or permanently, are liable to seek the use of comfort in food items.

Physiological Objective

This largely requires a mouth response but significantly an easy presence in the stomach of some weight.

Ritual/Timing

Because security is best constructed around routine, this will tend to occur at the same times in order to maximize the learnt behavioral support. So if one uses a Comfort product at the same time each day then the effect is cumulative and the mere thought of the Comfort item provides some serenity and security even without the actual eat.

Mood Journey

The journey is from any direction of stress or pressure through to calmness, heart rate reduction and a measure of inner peace.

Food Characteristics

Taste is not so important here and indeed strong taste is counterproductive.

Obviously, items such as milk and milky drinks work but so do foods that dissolve easily in the mouth, such as white bread and butter, biscuits and cakes that are not excessively flavored and carbohydrates in general. Mashed potato is very effective here.

The moment the taste becomes too pronounced and starts developing some interesting characteristic then the food is more appropriate for the classic indulgent product. Therefore the ideal is a bland variety of the same.

Needed Escape

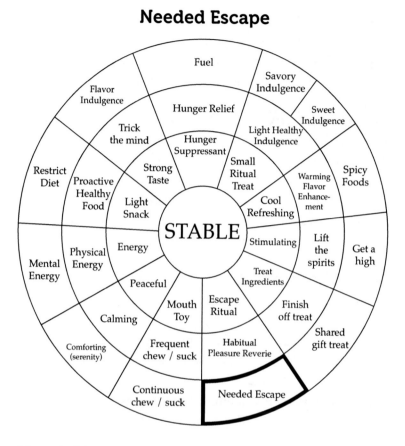

Mood Objective

This is a more desperate attempt to forget, move away from and distance oneself from unattractive worries or concerns.

Physiological Objective

Here the product needs to have some element of active ingredient.

Those products that produce relaxing responses also produce a physiological reaction which accelerates the awareness of emotional pain.

Ritual/Timing

This, unfortunately, is dangerously addictive and is observed by people using over-the-counter analgesics and other chemical products or alcohol in order to accelerate the process.

Mood Journey

This is a mood journey for which the end result is the only thing that counts.

The consumer wants to forget, distance themselves from the pressures and this requires active ingredients to be fully effective.

Food Characteristics (tastes and textures – their effect on mood)

Although this is a consumption it is not strictly speaking food, although some foods, chocolate and alcohol are exactly that.

This is not relevant to our efforts but is a good way of grasping the power of the needs of specific Need States.

Variation – Spicy or Cool

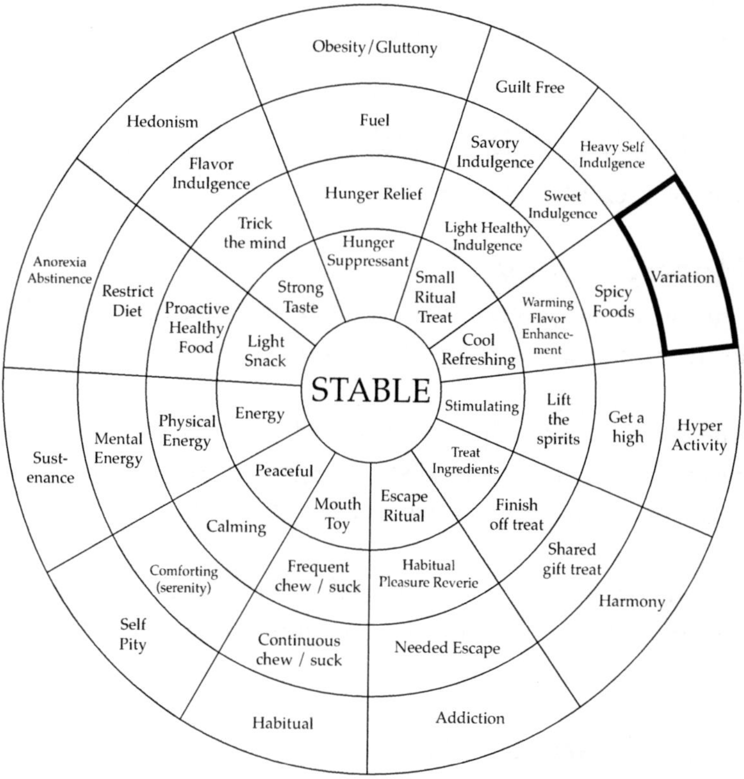

Circular diagram labels (outer to inner):

Obesity / Gluttony · Guilt Free · Hedonism · Fuel · Savory Indulgence · Heavy Self Indulgence · Flavor Indulgence · Hunger Relief · Sweet Indulgence · Trick the mind · Hunger Suppressant · Light Healthy Indulgence · Variation · Anorexia Abstinence · Restrict Diet · Proactive Healthy Food · Strong Taste · Small Ritual Treat · Warming Flavor Enhancement · Spicy Foods · Light Snack · Cool Refreshing · Energy · STABLE · Stimulating · Lift the spirits · Get a high · Hyper Activity · Physical Energy · Peaceful · Treat Ingredients · Sustenance · Mental Energy · Mouth Toy · Escape Ritual · Finish off treat · Calming · Frequent chew / suck · Habitual Pleasure Reverie · Shared gift treat · Comforting (serenity) · Harmony · Self Pity · Continuous chew / suck · Needed Escape · Habitual · Addiction

Mood Objective

With this rather esoteric Need State the objective is to consume something that is significantly away from the normal – either in its impact within the mouth or in its taste characteristic.

This is an infrequent consumption but can be very powerful.

Physiological Objective

The desire here is for differentiation and the power of taste characteristics and while the food can be consumed, actual ingredients can have a physiological effect.

Ritual/Timing

Here the desire is a different experience both in temperature or flavor and some sophisticated complex products do extremely well here.

Examples are powerful cheeses, red wines and esoteric foods such as shellfish and fungi.

Mood Journey

This is an alternative way of distancing oneself from the ordinary normal everyday consumption.

The pleasure is in the variation and the way in which this provides difference and distance – but it also needs to be relatively sophisticated to deliver that distance.

The mood journey often emanates from boredom and the requirement for something new through to a measure of prestigious individuality.

Food Characteristics

This food needs to be a step away from the norm, quite different and distinct, often expensive, but it does exist as an infrequent Need State.